Restoring Indigenous Self-Determination

Theoretical and Practical Approaches

EDITED BY
MARC WOONS

E-INTERNATIONAL
RELATIONS
PUBLISHING

E-International Relations
www.E-IR.info
Bristol, England
First published, 2014 (e-book)
New version, 2015 (e-book and print)

Copy Editing: Michael Pang
Production: Ran Xiao
Cover Image: valbel

ISBN 978-1-910814-03-1 (paperback)
ISBN 978-1-910814-07-9 (e-book)

A catalogue record for this book is available from the British Library

E-IR Edited Collections

Series Editors: Stephen McGlinchey, Marianna Karakoulaki and Robert L. Oprisko

E-IR's Edited Collections are open access scholarly books presented in a format that preferences brevity and accessibility while retaining academic conventions. Each book is available in print and e-book, and is published under a Creative Commons CC BY-NC 4.0 license. As E-International Relations is committed to open access in the fullest sense, free electronic versions of all of our books, including this one, are available on the E-International Relations website.

Find out more at: http://www.e-ir.info/publications

Recent titles

Nations under God: The Geopolitics of Faith in the Twenty-first Century

Popular Culture and World Politics: Theories, Methods, Pedagogies

Ukraine and Russia: People, Politics, Propaganda and Perspectives

Caliphates and Islamic Global Politics

Forthcoming

System, Society & the World: Exploring the English School (2nd Edition)

Environment, Climate Change and International Relations: Tendencies, Assessments and Perspectives

About the E-International Relations website

E-International Relations (www.E-IR.info) is the world's leading open access website for students and scholars of international politics. E-IR's daily publications feature expert articles, blogs, reviews and interviews – as well as a range of high quality student contributions. The website was established in November 2007 and now reaches over 200,000 unique visitors a month. E-IR is run by a registered non-profit organisation based in Bristol, England and staffed with an all-volunteer team.

Abstract

Indigenous peoples all over the world find themselves locked in power struggles with dominant states and transnational actors who resist their claims to land, culture, political recognition and other key factors associated with the idea of national self-determination. In the vast majority of cases, states and transnational corporations see such claims as barriers to the state-building projects that depend heavily on accessing and extracting resources from traditional Indigenous lands. In 2007, the importance of Indigenous self-determination alongside that of nation-states was significantly enhanced when, on September 13, the United Nations General Assembly adopted the Declaration on the Rights of Indigenous Peoples – suggesting that an important attitudinal shift might now be taking place internationally. Yet, as this volume's contributors suggest, much more work is needed in terms of, on the one hand, what Indigenous self-determination means in theory and, on the other hand, how it is to be achieved in practice.

Marc Woons is a Doctoral Fellow with the Research Foundation – Flanders (FWO) and Researcher at the KU Leuven's Research in Political Philosophy Leuven (RIPPLE) Institute. His work focuses on the intersection of power and justice in multinational contexts, with a particular focus on European Politics and Indigenous nationalism. His work has recently been featured in *Federal Governance, Settler Colonial Studies*, and *AlterNative: An International Journal of Indigenous Studies*, *St. Antony's International Review (Oxford)* and *Indigenous Policy Journal*.

Contents

The cover image depicts a traditional Sámi lávvu in Sápmi (in this case, in Troms county, Norway). The lávvu, a temporary and portable dwelling, plays an integral part in Sámi reindeer pastoralism. Its tremendous symbolic and cultural role was shown, for instance, when the Sámi built one on the steps of the Norwegian Parliament in Oslo during the Alta conflict, which took place in the late 1970s and early 1980s. The conflict resulted in the Norwegian state's greater recognition of the Sami's Indigenous rights. The lávvu also inspired the design of the Sámediggi (Sámi Parliament) in Kárášjohka, which opened in 1989.

Preface

JEFF CORNTASSEL

What are the sources of self-determining authority for Indigenous nations and peoples? How one responds to this question reveals competing narratives and worldviews relating to the self-determination discourse. State sources of self-determining authority are based on the Doctrine of Discovery (legal fiction that land occupied by non-Christians could be claimed as territory owned by the Crown) and other colonial myths of sovereignty, which are regularly challenged by Indigenous peoples living within and across state borders. After all, if one strips away the veneer of the Doctrine of Discovery, which is at the core of state legitimacy, states are left with little other than coercive measures and legal fictions in their often violent engagements with Indigenous nations. For the previously mentioned reasons, there is an urgency to the cross-comparative conversations in Woons' edited volume, which also serves as an important primer on the global self-determination discourse.

While the 2007 adoption of the United Nations Declaration on the Rights of Indigenous Peoples (UNDRIP) signalled a profound change for some (Henderson 2008; Anaya 2009), for others it offers new glimpses into ongoing processes of shape-shifting colonization via the rights discourse (White Face 2013; Kulchyski 2013) and the politics of recognition (Coulthard 2014). Ultimately, self-determination is something that is asserted and acted upon by Indigenous nations, and not negotiated into existence or offered freely by the state. Community-driven processes of reinvigoration and reconnection are key focal points for this important volume, which identifies and examines the contemporary scope and terrain of self-determination struggles worldwide.

According to the late Mohawk scholar, Patricia Monture-Angus (1999: 8), "... self-determination is principally, that is first and foremost, about relationships." For Indigenous nations and peoples, self-determining authority is grounded in the complex interrelationships between land, culture and community. One finds the roots of resurgence and sustainable self-determination in the daily actions of Indigenous nations honoring and fulfilling their inherent responsibilities. It is these everyday acts of resurgence, which coalesce around land-based governance, treaties, food sovereignty, language, extended kinship relations, restoration of land-based and water-based cultural practices,   etc., that renew Indigenous commitments to nurturing and honoring the relationships that promote the health and well-being of their communities. One cannot compartmentalize or simply focus on one dimension of self-determination without taking the other community-related factors into account. This is one reason why *Restoring Indigenous Self-Determination* widens its scope when discussing Indigenous self-determination in order to encompass questions of health and well-being as well as digital forms of self-determination.

Unfortunately, despite being formally renounced, the Doctrine of Discovery is still alive and well in state practice. Whether under the guise of globalization or the rights regime, colonial entities seek new ways to justify their encroachments onto Indigenous homelands via bioprospecting as well as extractive practices in the name of 'green energy'. Fortunately, for every new iteration of the colonial Doctrine of Discovery, Indigenous peoples have their own version of a *Doctrine of Recovery*. An Indigenous Doctrine of Recovery operates on at least two levels as: 1) place-based peoples and communities seeking recovery *from* the trauma of ongoing colonial violence; and, 2) simultaneously promoting the recovery *of* Indigenous knowledge and practices through reconnections with land, culture and community. So I challenge readers to fully engage with the theoretical concepts and practices presented in this edited volume, such as anti-extractivism and Abya Yala, and begin to understand how Indigenous peoples' lives and self-determining authority extend far beyond that of the state.

References

Anaya, S.J. (2009). "The Right of Indigenous Peoples to Self-determination in the Post-Declaration Era." In *Making the Declaration Work: The United Nations Declaration on the Rights of Indigenous Peoples*, edited by Claire Charters and Rodolfo Stavenhagen, 184–198. Copenhagen: International Work Group for Indigenous Affairs.

Coulthard, G. (2014). *Red Skin, White Masks*. Minneapolis: University of Minnesota Press.

Henderson, J. (2008). *Indigenous Diplomacy and the Rights of Peoples: Achieving UN recognition*. Saskatoon: Purich Publishing.

Kulchyski, P. (2013). *Aboriginal Rights Are Not Human Rights*. Winnipeg: ARP Books.

Monture-Angus, P. (1999). *Journeying Forward: Dreaming of First Nations' Independence*. Halifax: Fernwood Publishing.

White Face, C. (2013). *Indigenous Nations Rights in the Balance: An Analysis of the Declaration on the Rights of Indigenous Peoples*. St. Paul: Living Justice Press

Introduction

On the Meaning of Restoring Indigenous Self-Determination

MARC WOONS

KU LEUVEN, BELGIUM

What does it mean *to restore*? The *Oxford English Dictionary* (1989) offers over a dozen definitions. Almost all are used within Indigenous self-determination discussions in one way or another, in good ways and in bad ways. The different meanings of the word, I suggest, belong to four definitional categories that help explain what restoring Indigenous self-determination is, and is not, about.

Before looking at each in turn, it is important to recognize that Indigenous self-determination is not something that has been lost or destroyed. Instead, centuries of colonization has set in motion events and created circumstances that have forced Indigenous peoples to adapt in how they assert their authority to self-determine within their homelands. Though I expand on what this might mean, restoring Indigenous self-determination broadly encompasses many approaches pursued within and against modern states that all too often perpetuate colonialism by ignoring – or even promoting – its logic and effects. The idea that states should recognize Indigenous nations fails to go far enough time and again. Sometimes it is even used to co-opt or promote inadequate compromises that fall short of the full implications of what justice entails. Thus, restoring Indigenous self-determination must also – or primarily – be about Indigenous peoples asserting themselves and promoting healing from within.

The first definition speaks foremost of the need to make it as if nothing ever happened by giving something back: "to return to the original position", "to bring into existence again," or "to bring back to the original state." Let's call this the *return* definition. A second definition recognizes how idealistic this can often be, suggesting instead that we strive "to bring it as nearly as possible to its original form" while acknowledging a residual need "to compensate." This is the *restitution* definition. Still an effort to give back, it recognizes that things have changed, making it either unfeasible or undesirable to return to the original state. The third and fourth definitional categories speak to moral motives for returning or pursuing restitution. One speaks to those whose actions established a need "to set right", which in the most serious of cases is necessary "to free [themselves] from the effects of sin." I call this the *reconciliation* definition, emphasizing a duty to take rectifying action. The final category speaks to addressing the intended recipient's resulting predicament, suggesting that it is imperative "to revive", "to bring back mental calm", "to reinstate ... dignity", "to bring ... back to a healthy or vigorous state." Let's call this the *reinvigorate* definition.

A transitive verb, to restore also requires answers to questions like "what" and "who". Within this volume, self-determination answers the former question. Article 3 of the United Nations (UN) Declaration on the Rights of Indigenous Peoples (UNDRIP), adopted in 2007, states that "Indigenous peoples have the right to self-determination. By virtue of that right they freely determine their political status and freely pursue their economic, social and cultural development" (UN General Assembly 2008). It affirms a *political* claim previously extended only to (nation-)states in the analogous, and original, UN definition found in article 1, part 2 of the UN Charter (1945), which says: "To develop friendly relations among nations based on respect for the principle of equal rights and self-determination of peoples, and to take other appropriate measures to strengthen universal peace" (United Nations 1945). Yet, when the self-determination of states and that of Indigenous nations clash, as they typically do, the UNDRIP's article 46 suggests that the territorial integrity of the former be maintained at the expense of the latter (White Face and Wobaga 2013). Most notably, article 46 states, "Nothing in this Declaration may be interpreted as implying for any State, people, group or person any right to engage in any activity or to perform any act contrary to the Charter of the United Nations or construed as authorizing or encouraging any action which would dismember or impair, totally or in part, the territorial integrity or political unity of sovereign and independent States" (UN General Assembly 2008). Thus, the ability of Indigenous nations to use UNDRIP to challenge the power imbalance they are locked into with states has been truncated.

The "who" speaks to what it means to be Indigenous. Taiaiake Alfred and Jeff Corntassel believe that Indigenous peoples around the world – despite differing histories, socio-economic, and political positions – are united in "the struggle to survive as distinct peoples on foundations constituted in their unique heritages, attachments to their homelands, and natural ways of life ... as well as the fact that their existence[1] is in large part lived as determined acts of survival against colonizing states' efforts to eradicate them culturally, politically and physically" (Alfred and Corntassel 2005: 597). The oppositional and political claims uniting Indigenous peoples, in short, stem largely from a shared desire to address historical *and ongoing* injustices committed in the name of imperialism, colonialism, and other forms of domination perpetuated around the world. In response to these challenges, Thomas King succinctly describes the goal: "The fact of Native existence is that we live *modern* lives informed by *traditional* values and contemporary realities and that *we wish to live those lives on our terms*" (King 2012: 302, my emphasis).

So, does restoring Indigenous self-determination mean to return, to restitute, to reconcile, or to reinvigorate? In principle it can mean all four, though in practice they are never applied in equal measure because of differing political circumstances. The idea of return, taken literally, is generally weaker than the idea of restitution. Despite the fact that some scholars incorrectly believe most Indigenous peoples want to return to an unattainable past (e.g., Cairns 2000), the opposite is much closer to the truth. Most are astutely aware that time only moves forward and that self-determination will invariably look different now and into the future than it did before external interference took place. King, to use the example at hand, focuses on living *modern* lives that *honour* past traditions and values. This is very different than trying to live in the past. We will never return to a time when Indigenous peoples clearly lived on one side of the river, ocean or mountain and non-Indigenous peoples on the other. Colonisation and imperialism's impacts cannot simply be reversed, so we have to move forward by identifying and challenging ongoing injustices (Tesoriero and Ife 2006; Hall 2006). Yet, the idea of return does have a conceptual place in the discussion. For instance, centuries of colonialism may have left its mark on Indigenous lands so that they can't be returned in the original condition, control over the land can be returned. Such control may not always equate to total autonomy, but following the principle of returning Indigenous priority is indeed possible.

The idea of restitution might do better to reflect colonialism's lasting and irreversible impacts. Yet, it raises serious questions. What are the reasons for restitution? What would fair restitution entail? Who should receive restitution? How would it be determined? The list of questions is a lengthy one. Here, very different perspectives emerge between Indigenous and non-Indigenous peoples. Whereas the former assert their inherent authority to self-determine, demand self-determination as a right, demand recognition of prior sovereignty, and demand respect for historical agreements, the latter typically believe that these claims should be reduced in favour of more limited state recognition and greater forms of redistribution in the form of funding or access to state programs. In other words, the non-Indigenous majority controlling the state often expects Indigenous peoples to forego the full normative implications of their claims and to accept forms of assimilation into state institutions as forms of restitution. To the extent that this is promoted, Indigenous self-determination is denied. It would seem that a more just starting point would require greater consideration of what Indigenous peoples themselves view as fair in cases where disagreement prevails given that it is they who have been disempowered. In such cases, even the existence of the state itself as the arbiter of claims and dispenser of recognition is rightfully questioned.

The disconnect between what colonial states propose and what Indigenous self-determination requires can be at least partially explained by the third and fourth definitional categories, which speak to moral motivations. Against arguments to the contrary, settler majorities typically find reason to minimize their obligations toward Indigenous peoples. Their general self-interest cuts against the idea of setting things right or freeing the state from the effects of sin, to paraphrase the earlier definition. Most contemporary settlers, who benefit from colonial histories that saw them gain land at the expense of Indigenous peoples, believe that they should not pay for the deeds of their ancestors. For instance, Canadian courts have at times gone quite far in promoting moral arguments that support Indigenous self-determination and access to traditional territories, but politicians typically respond by dragging their feet and doing as little as possible (e.g., see Harty and Murphy 2005; Hoehn 2012). Settler populations generally find ways of convincing themselves that no sins have been committed or that time has closed old wounds. On the whole, this affirms for Indigenous peoples that they simply can't expect dominant states to act without pressure, whether through state institutions, civil actions, or international pressure. This is not to say that a sense of moral obligation never exists on the part of states, but that even when it does it typically falls far short of full and equal self-determination for Indigenous peoples.

The idea of reinvigoration comes closest to the heart of what it means to restore Indigenous self-determination, giving the other definitions vigour and a sense of direction and purpose. It is beyond doubt that state- and nation-building efforts have marginalized and ultimately sought to destroy many of the Indigenous nations present in all regions of the world. Beyond the need for dominant groups to cleanse themselves of the effects of historical and ongoing injustices is the paramount need to "bring back a healthy and vigorous state" for every Indigenous person and within all Indigenous communities. Restoring the health and well-being of Indigenous communities involves breaking free from the various forms of dependency – financial, psychological, physical – created by colonialism and colonial institutions (Alfred 2009). Though external support and respect can make a tremendous difference, another aspect is positive transformation and decolonization within the communities themselves. This requires aspects of the previous three definitions, but should not be limited to them. Clearly, expecting non-Indigenous peoples to support the steps necessary to revitalize Indigenous communities, especially when it threatens their own self-interest and perception of the world, seems an unlikely avenue. Therefore, Indigenous peoples are all too often forced to focus on asserting their claims – rooted in principles of equal self-determination, prior occupancy of lands, and colonial histories – primarily outside existing state and global institutions. Although this sometimes leads states to respond using violence, the act of resisting itself – apart from the small and not so small victories – seems to help reinvigorate people individually and collectively. This is primarily because assimilating or waiting in vain both fail as options that provide any form of restoration understood as reinvigoration. In summary, we all have a role to play in reinvigorating Indigenous peoples, though how this will come about remains an open question.

The idea of restoring Indigenous self-determination clearly involves complex and inter-related debates about what self-determination means and how states and Indigenous peoples can take the steps necessary for achieving it. It also involves debates about the many facets just discussed on why self-determination is required and how we can usher in a new era where Indigenous peoples once again enjoy the same freedoms currently enjoyed only by dominant nations who monopolize access to lands, resources, and institutional power through state and, increasingly, international institutions like the World Bank, International Monetary Fund, and so on. In other words, it requires looking at the many ways that the idea of restoring plays out politically through returning – or promoting restitution for – what continues to be taken from Indigenous peoples. It involves promoting justice-based arguments that will awaken non-Indigenous peoples to the historical realities at the same time as Indigenous peoples continue to assert themselves and revitalize their communities at all levels and through a variety of channels, including those that come from within.

The above is purely an introduction to the types of issues covered within this volume. It is only the tip of an iceberg that is more thoroughly described by the dozen contributors who provide clearer answers to who is Indigenous, what it means to restore Indigenous self-determination, and why it is important. Most use specific examples from different parts of the world to highlight the various theoretical issues raised as Indigenous struggles evolve in different contexts. All the authors seem to challenge, in one way or another, the state-centric model and its strong tendency to marginalize and exclude Indigenous peoples from their lands and the political processes affecting them. The ultimate purpose of this volume is to share ideas on how to restore greater balance so that Indigenous peoples around the world find their place among an international community that recognizes and respects their differences and treats them as equal members. With this shared focus at the forefront of the volume, it is an honour to introduce the twelve papers within this volume that I believe highlight many paths that can take us there.

This publication begins with Ravi de Costa's overview of the different ways states define who is Indigenous. In looking at state policies from every continent, he points out three general patterns that sometimes coexist. In some cases, states use culture or descent, while in other cases they provide greater space for self-definition. Though the latter is more in line with principles of self-determination, he suggests that there does not appear to be a trend in this direction, at least that can be separated from the more overarching need to reconstruct Indigenous-state relations.

Manuela L. Picq examines the relationship between Indigenous politics and International Relations (IR) through the lens of anti-extractivist movements. Drawing primarily on South American examples, she suggests that greater consideration must be given to the place of such movements within IR debates. Whereas extractivist states typically overlook or seek to minimize Indigenous land claims, arguing that such lands are empty and therefore exploitable, Indigenous anti-extractivist assertions rooted in self-determination reveal the limits of the state-centric model, both in theory and in practice. In that sense, Indigenous claims to self-determination call for a reconceptualization of disciplinary canons that perpetuate Westphalian notions of sovereignty.

In his piece, Michael Murphy studies the link between self-determination and Indigenous health and well-being. To show that there is a strong possibility that such a connection exists, he draws on recent empirical studies that suggest people who do not have control over their own lives tend to have poorer health outcomes. Consequently, restricting Indigenous self-determination both causes and sustains tremendous health disparities between Indigenous peoples and the non-Indigenous peoples they live alongside.

Tim Rowse's contribution investigates how Indigenous peoples adapt within contexts not of their own making. Studying the last two centuries of Aborigine-state relations in Australia, Rowse looks at the changing ways Aborigines have envisioned their futures over time and how, in certain instances, what seemed like positive steps actually limited Indigenous autonomy and development. This leads him to conclude that greater awareness of historical processes is vital to promote a vision of self-determination understood as self-transformation, whereby Indigenous peoples can more freely promote their interests as they regain access to traditional territories.

Marisa Elena Duarte challenges the idea that Indigenous peoples are have-nots in using information and communication technologies (ICTs). She highlights examples where Indigenous peoples use ICTs to develop their own transnational networks and use existing information and technologies to further self-determination and Native ways of knowing. In this way, a greater understanding of the relationship between Indigenous knowledge and the use of ICTs sheds light on what self-determination means in our globalizing world.

Using the case of the Māori, the Indigenous inhabitants of what is more commonly known as New Zealand, Dominic O'Sullivan defends a "liberal theory of indigeneity" rooted in Nancy Fraser's idea of "participatory parity." Such a theory would grant the Māori greater influence in shaping the shared public life of the state at the same time as granting them greater forms of autonomy. This is in contrast to "biculturalism," the predominant view existing within New Zealand since the 1980s, which O'Sullivan believes has not protected the Māori against the "tyranny of the majority" or extended autonomy to its full reasonable extent. The "liberal theory of indigeneity" provides an alternative that better distributes power and authority within the state in a more inclusive manner.

Roderic Pitty discusses the reluctance that states have in implementing the UNDRIP, suggesting that it has so far proven to be a symbolic moral gesture which has yet to change relations of domination. Drawing on the highly influential idea of self-determination understood as relational autonomy or non-domination (as opposed to non-interference), an idea most notably put forth by Iris Marion Young and akin to Nancy Fraser's idea of participatory parity mentioned in the previous article, Pitty believes that third-parties need to be used in difficult cases, such as in Australia (as well as Canada, New Zealand, and the United States), where states refuse to seek Indigenous consent for state-wide institutions by renegotiating the political relationship. This rests on the belief that progress is directly related to the amount of external pressure placed on states.

Also introducing the idea of relational self-determination, Else Grete Broderstad develops a four-stage framework for understanding and evaluating greater forms of self-determination granted to the Sāmi in Northern Norway. She shows how each step brought the Sāmi closer to realizing a relational vision of self-determination whereby they gained more effective forms of decision-making alongside the non-Sāmi majority in shared decision-making institutions, and greater forms of institutional autonomy, primarily through the creation of the Sāmi Parliament. Though there is still some way to go, political participation in various institutions – including the international – is required to promote greater dialogue and agreement between the Sāmi and the Norwegian state.

Hassan O. Kaya, in his piece, questions the proper place of external knowledge systems in African indigenous societies and environments. He urges Africans to resist the quick solution of importing Western knowledge systems, which often leads to solutions that are inappropriate or insensitive to local needs and conditions. Instead, important local issues like environmental sustainability demand that African Indigenous Knowledge Systems are strengthened and spread through educational institutions that foster positive interactions with imported knowledge systems.

In the first of two articles on Tibet and its Indigenous people, Michael Davis outlines inconsistencies with the People's Republic of China's position. On the one hand, they voted to support the UNDRIP in 2007. On the other, they declared that no Indigenous peoples lived within China's borders. Davis points out inconsistencies within China's position by looking at not just the contents of the UNDRIP, but also agreements between China and Tibet, as well as their own internal documents and standards in recognizing autonomous regions like Hong Kong. Davis believes China has taken a strong colonial position with respect to Tibet, fuelling international skepticism about China's rise.

Rob Dickinson's article on Tibet focuses on understanding why Tibet has had so little success in promoting greater self-determination for its people. He notes that successful self-determination movements, such as in Kosovo and Bangladesh, seemed to require levels of violent rebellion that Tibetans refuse to pursue. Moreover, the international community seems less willing in the Tibetan case to face China because of its increasing strength, leading to a vastly different outcome than in places like Egypt or Libya. He mentions new possibilities offered by social media, though this does not seem capable of compensating for a lack of international support.

The Publication closes with Emilio del Valle Escalante's introduction to the concept of Abya Yala and two movements that seek to promote its aims. Abya Yala refers both to the entire continent of America, and speaks to the need for Indigenous self-expression as a means of counteracting centuries of imperialism, colonialism, and domination. The Zapatistas are the subject of the first case, highlighting an example of an Indigenous struggle that rejects electoral politics and directly asserts the need for greater autonomy from the nation-state and its colonial biases. The second example is that of the Movement Toward Socialism in Bolivia, which successfully pursued electoral politics when Evo Morales was elected President in 2006. In the final case, President Morales has struggled to steer a path free of colonial biases. Despite their differences del Valle Escalante believes that both cases highlight important debates and struggles that are necessary to achieve Indigenous self-determination in the Abya Yala project.

References

Alfred, T. (2009) "Colonialism and State Dependency." *Journal of Aboriginal Health,* 5(2): 42–60.

Alfred, T. and Corntassel, J. (2005) "Being Indigenous: Resurgences against Contemporary Colonialism." *Government and Opposition*, 40(4): 597–614.

Cairns, A.C. (2000) *Citizens Plus: Aboriginal Peoples and the Canadian State*. Vancouver, British Columbia: University of British Columbia Press.

Hall, S. (1996) "When was 'the post-colonial'? Thinking at the limit." In: Chambers, I. and Curti, L. eds. *The Post-Colonial Question: Common Skies, Divided Horizons*. London: Routledge.

Harty, S. and Murphy, M. (2005) *In Defence of Multinational Citizenship*. Cardiff, UK: University of Wales Press.

Hoehn, F. (2012) *Reconciling Sovereignties: Aboriginal Nations and Canada*. Saskatoon, Saskatchewan: Native Law Centre, University of Saskatchewan.

King, T. (2012) *The Inconvenient Indian: A Curious Account of Native Peoples in North America*. Toronto: Doubleday.

Oxford English Dictionary. (1989) 2nd ed. Oxford: Oxford University Press.

Tesoriero, F. and Ife, J. (2006) *Community Development: Community-based Alternatives in an Age of Globalization*. 3rd ed. Upper Saddle River, New Jersey: Pearson Education.

White Face, C. and Wobaga, Z. (2013) *Indigenous Nations' Rights in the Balance: An Analysis of the Declaration on the Rights of Indigenous Peoples*. St. Paul, Minnesota: Living Justice Press.

United Nations. (1945) *Charter of the United Nations and Statute of the International Court of Justice*. San Francisco, California: United Nations.

UN General Assembly. (2008) *United Nations Declaration on the Rights of Indigenous Peoples resolution / adopted by the General Assembly*. 2 October 2007, UN. Doc. A/RES/61/295.

Endnotes

[1]   On the same page, Alfred and Corntassel describe this as a place-based existence. Speaking to the critical importance of this dimension, they state, "it is this oppositional, place-based existence, along with the consciousness of being in struggle against the dispossessing and demeaning fact of colonization by foreign peoples, that fundamentally distinguishes Indigenous peoples from other peoples of the world" (Alfred and Corntassel 2005: 597).

1

Self-Determination and State Definitions of Indigenous Peoples

RAVI DE COSTA
YORK UNIVERSITY, CANADA

This article takes up several themes of the volume through a consideration of the ways that states define Indigenous peoples in law and administrative practice. It is based on an unfolding project that seeks to provide a comprehensive survey of state practice. Currently, it draws on a study of over 20 states in all regions of the world. These definitions are highly variable, while at the same time they reveal certain consistencies that are driven by both historical choices and persistent cultural assumptions.

Of course, the core of this volume is Indigenous self-determination. The continuation of colonial and often arbitrary systems of state definition is irreconcilable with any serious understanding of self-determination; this is even more relevant since the passage of the United Nations Declaration on the Rights of Indigenous Peoples (UNDRIP) (UN General Assembly 2008). Systems of definition create regimes in which states both apportion entitlements to Indigenous persons and communities – including specific welfare and social policy measures, land rights, and distinct political or electoral status – as well as subject them to specific rules. The specific histories of these regimes originate in the administrative needs of colonial powers, not those of Indigenous communities themselves. As such, these are now institutions that simultaneously promote and constrain Indigenous self-determination (Povinelli 2002; Merlan 2009). A paradox of late colonialism is that many of these rules have been devolved to Indigenous communities themselves, such that decisions over *membership*, if not *definition*, are, in some places, now in their own hands.

At a high level of generalization, we can see three broad characteristics with which state definition practices and regimes might be explained. These are: the use of varied notions of *culture*, including a range of environmental and economic practices; the idea of *descent* from a population clearly identified and recorded at an earlier time; and the already mentioned recent shift to systems where communities have control over membership. Often community control over membership reinforces earlier systems of definition based on descent or cultural attributes. The following examples of these characteristics are drawn from a much longer work, in which the context of each state is more fully provided, with some states employing multiple and overlapping approaches (de Costa 2014).

The use of "culture" as a defining characteristic of sub-state populations is not a straightforward matter. In the contemporary world, the effects of human mobility and inter-marriage, as well as socio-cultural change, make many strict criteria seem archaic at best, racist and absurd at worst. In many cases, they attempt to offer simple and static categorizations for complex and dynamic social realities. This is the case in the Scandinavian countries, where Sámi status is partly determined by the use of Sámi language in the home; other entitlements in Norway and Sweden are reserved for those whose livelihoods rely in part on reindeer herding (Norway 1987; Sweden 1992).

Several other states use economic criteria, such as Kenya, where an Indigenous community "has retained and maintained a traditional lifestyle and livelihood based on a hunter or gatherer economy" (Kenya 2010: 162–3). Taiwan's Indigenous Peoples Basic Law envisages communities "[h]unting wild animals; Collecting wild plants and fungus; Collecting minerals, rocks and soils; Utilising water resources… [all of which] can only be conducted for traditional culture, ritual or self-consumption" (Taiwan 2001).

Latin American countries have adopted definitions that appear more attentive to the particularity of Indigenous identities and are more at ease with the concept of "pluri-national" states. Bolivia's constitution, for example, describes the shared "world vision" of the "Indigenous peasant nation"; in Guatemala, as part of the conclusion to the country's conflict in May 1995, an agreement was reached between the Government of Guatemala and the guerrillas of the Unidad Revolucionaria Nacional Guatemalteca that set out the Mayan peoples' "world vision… based in the harmonious relations of all elements in the universe" (Guatemala 1995; Sieder 2011: 252–4). Numerous Latin American states – like Mexico, Peru, Colombia, Bolivia, and Ecuador – draw into their definitions of Indigenous peoples' rights and identities a recognition of existing or traditional Indigenous political orders and authorities that have governed specific territories.

Some states maintain unreconstructed views of Indigenous peoples as isolated anachronisms. Russia's defining law speaks of "numerically-small indigenous peoples" and creates an arbitrary upper population limit of 50,000 people (Shapovalov 2005). India's definition of "scheduled tribes" places them in a broader category of "backward classes," and its Ministry of Tribal Affairs uses administrative criteria that include "primitive traits, distinctive culture, geographical isolation, shyness of contact with the community at large, and backwardness" (India n.d.).

However, numerous states use relative criteria, defining Indigenous peoples based on certain differences from a putative mainstream population. Indigenous peoples in the United States seeking recognition as "federally recognized Indian tribes" need to establish a continuity of distinctiveness and autonomy (Quinn 1990). Brazil's agency for Indigenous peoples, the Fundação Nacional do Índio, draws its idea of indigeneity partly using a relation to non-indigenous communities, such that an Indigenous person is "any individual Indian recognised as a member for a pre-Columbian community who identifies and is considered so by the Brazilian (i.e., non-Indian) population with whom they are in contact" (Brazil n.d.).

Possibly the most common feature of state definitions is the relational quality of priority: that a given Indigenous community will be able to trace its history to the time before the arrival of a colonial power and a settler society. Of course, this is not a definition based in culture, but in descent.

States that rely on descent include the United States, which has a highly bureaucratized system that uses "base rolls," enumerations of Indigenous populations done in the 19th and early 20th centuries, from which contemporary adjudications of status are determined (Thornton 1997; Gover 2011). These were contentious at the time and now give rise to elaborate and sometimes divisive regimes which measure "blood quantum" to determine membership (Garroutte 2003). Canada is quite similar to this model, having begun to enumerate Indigenous people from the 1850s; in place now is a regime defining "registered" or "status Indians" (Canada 2013). This system has been revised significantly as social norms evolved. Litigation since the 1980s has sought to remove gender discrimination, by which an Indigenous woman and her children were discriminated against if she "married out," though this remains a source of controversy (Grammond 2009).

Some states have dabbled with even more scientific approaches to descent. For example, the states of Vermont, in the United States, and Tasmania, in Australia, both proposed genetic testing of Indigenous peoples (Gardiner-Garden 2003). Such approaches are highly resisted and there is strong global opposition to the documenting of Indigenous peoples' DNA for purposes such as the documenting of the history of human evolution (Harry 2013).

The devolution of definition systems is also now established in numerous states. Quite often this is the result of comprehensive negotiations between states and specific Indigenous communities at different historical periods, resulting in treaties and final agreements (Gover 2011). This is true in parts of the "settler states" of the United States, New Zealand, Australia, and Canada. Such negotiations, by bracketing lands and resources for specific Indigenous communities, appear to have created incentives for those communities to delimit their populations in ways that reproduce strong or exclusionary notions of descent and/or culture.

Numerous states incorporate the need for Indigenous individuals to self-identify as well as to be recognized by an Indigenous community. This is the case in Australia, though such communities themselves are understood primarily in terms of descent (Australia 1986). Indeed the interaction of the categories of cultural difference and descent in states' determination of who is entitled to resources or services is a recurrent part of Indigenous life today.

A key question for both states and Indigenous peoples is how to respond to the dynamism of contemporary Indigenous life, given the sedimentary effects of centuries of colonial population management. In many settler states, histories of child removal and community dislocation have resulted in recent efforts to reconnect individuals to their communities and identities with concomitant effects on population numbers; birth rates in many Indigenous communities are frequently much higher than amongst the neighbouring or dominant societies. In an era of global austerity and neoliberal social policies, these phenomena create incentives for states to continue devolving membership rules while maintaining or reducing resources per capita; it places communities under great pressure to exclude and more vigorously police their own borders.

A persistent question about globalization is its assumed tendency to homogenize, erasing local variety and difference. One scholar has suggested that there is an inevitable trajectory which will see the growth of self-definition and thereby variety (Beach 2007); this is an expectation of numerous articles in UNDRIP, which, though it provides no definition, has much to say about the power of definition (UN General Assembly 2008).

Article 3 of the Declaration endorses Indigenous peoples' rights of self-determination, and subsequent articles declare that this encompasses the rights to autonomy and self-governance, to their own political institutions, and to a nationality. Article 9 prohibits discrimination against Indigenous peoples' right to belong to an Indigenous community, "in accordance with the traditions and customs of the community or nation concerned". Articles 18-20 entrench a right to Indigenous institutions. Most critically, Article 33 provides that "Indigenous peoples have the right to determine their own identity or membership in accordance with their customs and traditions. This does not impair the right of indigenous individuals to obtain citizenship of the States in which they live... Indigenous peoples have the right to determine the structures and to select the membership of their institutions in accordance with their own procedures." In the aspirations set out in UNDRIP and endorsed by most states, there would seem to be little role for the state in *defining* who is or is not an Indigenous person.

In another work, I have examined early signs of states' adoption of UNDRIP principles (de Costa 2011). However, what this ongoing survey of states across all inhabited continents and regions is revealing is a patchwork of practices that are shaped by the specific local histories in each territory, colony, and state, as well as the relative political power of the Indigenous communities in each territory. States use both criteria of descent and cultural difference, with some giving greater weight to communities themselves in regulating their own memberships. It is, though, far from evident that there is an emerging and inevitable trend for states to completely devolve the power to define Indigenous peoples to those peoples affected. Autonomy over legal and political identities for Indigenous peoples is likely to come as part of a complete reconstruction of Indigenous-state relations, and not prior to such an occurrence.

References

Australia. Australian Law Reform Commission. (1986) *Recognition of Aboriginal Customary Laws*. Canberra: Publishing Service. Available at: http://www.austlii.edu.au/au/other/alrc/publications/reports/31/ (Accessed 11 January 2014).

Beach, H. (2007) "Self-determining the Self: Aspects of Saami Identity Management in Sweden." *Acta Borealia,* 24(1): 1–25.

Brazil. Fundação Nacional do Índio (n.d.) *Povos Indígenas. O que é ser índio.* Available at: http://www.funai.gov.br/indios/conteudo.htm#SER_INDIO (Accessed 11 Janaury 2014).

Canada. Aboriginal Affairs and Northern Development Canada. (2013) *Indian Status*. Available at: https://www.aadnc-aandc.gc.ca/eng/1100100032374/1100100032378 (Accessed 11 January 2014).

de Costa, R. (2014) "State's definitions of Indigenous peoples: A survey of practices."

In: Berg-Nordlie, M., Saglie, J, and Sullivan, A. eds. *Indigenous Politics: Institutions, Representation, Mobilisation*. Colchester, United Kingdom: ECPR Press.

de Costa, R. (2011) "Implementing UNDRIP: Developments and possibilities." *Prairie Forum,* 36(Fall): 55–77.

Gardiner-Garden, J. (2003) *Defining Aboriginality in Australia*. Canberra: Department of the Parliamentary Library.

Garroutte, E.M. (2003) *Real Indians: identity and the survival of Native America.* Berkeley, California: University of California Press.

Gover, K. (2011) *Tribal constitutionalism: states, tribes, and the governance of membership*. Oxford: Oxford University Press.

Grammond, S. (2009) *Identity captured by law: membership in Canada's indigenous peoples and linguistic minorities.* Montréal and Kingston: McGill-Queen's University Press.

Guatemala. (1995) *Agreement on the Identity and Rights of Indigenous Peoples*. Washington, District of Columbia: United States Institute of Peace. Available at: http://www.usip.org/sites/default/files/file/resources/collections/peace_agreements/guat_950331.pdf (Accessed 11 January 2014).

Harry, D. (2013) "Indigenous peoples and gene disputes." *Chicago-Kent Law Review,* 84(1): 147–96.

India. Ministry of Tribal Affairs. (n.d.). *Definition – Article 342 Scheduled Tribes.* Available at: http://www.tribal.nic.in/Content/DefinitionpRrofiles.aspx (Accessed 11 January 2014).

Kenya. (2010) *The Constitution of Kenya*. Nairobi: National Council for Law Reporting.

Merlan, F. (2009) "Indigeneity: Global and Local." *Current Anthropology,* 50(3): 303–33.

Norway. (1987) *Act of 12 June 1987 No. 56 concerning the Sameting (the Sami parliament) and other Sami legal matters (the Sami Act)*. Available at: http://www.regjeringen.no/en/doc/laws/Acts/the-sami-act-.html?id=449701 (Accessed 11 January 2014).

Povinelli, E.A. (2002) *The Cunning of Recognition: Indigenous Alterities and the Making of Australian Multiculturalism*. Durham, North Carolina: Duke University Press.

Shapovalov, A. (2005) "Straightening Out the Backward Legal Regulation of 'Backward' Peoples' Claims to Land in the Russian North: The Concept of Indigenous Neomodernism." *Georgetown International Environmental Law Review,* 17(3): 435–69.

Sieder, R. (2011) "'Emancipation' or 'Regulation'? Law, Globalization and Indigenous Peoples' Rights in Post-war Guatemala." *Economy and Society,* 40(2): 239-65.

Sweden. (1992) *Sami Parliament Act*. Available at: http://www.sametinget.se/9865 (Accessed 11 January 2014).

Taiwan. Council of Indigenous peoples (2001) *Status Act for Indigenous Peoples*. Available at: http://www.apc.gov.tw/portal/docDetail. html?CID=74DD1F415708044AandDID=3E651750B400646776702AECEC7630DD (Accessed 11 January 2014).

Thornton, R. (1997) "Tribal Membership Requirements and the Demography of 'Old' and 'New' Native Americans." *Population Research and Policy Review,* 16(1-2): 33–42.

UN General Assembly. (2008) United Nations Declaration on the Rights of Indigenous Peoples resolution / adopted by the General Assembly. 2 October 2007, UN. Doc. A/ RES/61/295.

2

Self-Determination as Anti-Extractivism: How Indigenous Resistance Challenges World Politics

MANUELA L. PICQ
UNIVERSIDAD SAN FRANCISCO DE QUITO, ECUADOR

Indigeneity is an unusual way to think about International Relations (IR). Most studies of world politics ignore Indigenous perspectives, which are rarely treated as relevant to thinking about the international (Shaw 2008; Beier 2009). Yet Indigenous peoples are engaging in world politics with a dynamism and creativity that defies the silences of our discipline (Morgan 2011). In Latin America, Indigenous politics has gained international legitimacy, influencing policy for over two decades (Cott 2008; Madrid 2012). Now, Indigenous political movements are focused on resisting extractive projects on autonomous territory from the Arctic to the Amazon (Banerjee 2012; Sawyer and Gómez 2012). Resistance has led to large mobilized protests, invoked international law, and enabled alternative mechanisms of authority. In response, governments have been busy criminalizing Indigenous claims to consultation that challenge extractive models of development. Indigenous opposition to extractivism ultimately promotes self-determination rights, questioning the states' authority over land by placing its sovereignty into historical context. In that sense, Indigeneity is a valuable approach to understanding world politics as much as it is a critical concept to move beyond state-centrism in the study of IR.

The Consolidation of Indigenous Resistance against Extractivism

Indigenous peoples are contesting extractive projects in various, complementary ways. Collective marches have multiplied as an immediate means of resistance throughout the Americas. In 2012, the Confederation of

Indigenous Nationalities of Ecuador led thousands of people on a 15-day, 400-mile March for Life, Water, and the Dignity of Peoples, demanding a new water law, the end of open-pit mining, and a stop to the expansion of oil concessions. Within days, a similar mobilization took over Guatemala City. The Indigenous, Peasant, and Popular March in Defense of Mother Earth covered 212 kilometers to enter the capital with nearly 15,000 people protesting mining concessions, hydroelectric plants, and evictions. In Bolivia, various marches demanded consultation as the government prepared to build a highway within the Indigenous Territory and National Park Isidoro Sécure (TIPNIS). From Canada's Idle No More movement to the protests against damming the Xingú River Basin in Brazil, Indigenous movements are rising and demanding they be allowed to participate in decisions affecting their territories.

Protests are at the core of global Indigenous agendas. In 2013, the Fifth Continental Summit of Indigenous Peoples of the Abya Yala encouraged communities to step-up resistance in light of the threat posed by state-sponsored extractivism. This is what Indigenous women were doing when they walked from Amazon territories to Quito, Ecuador, denouncing government plans to drill without consultation in the Yasuní reserve. Local protests are not trivial or irrelevant in world politics. Rather, they are part of a larger effort to transform local concerns into international politics.

Indigenous peoples have remarkable expertise in international law and are savvily leveraging their rights to consultation and self-determination guaranteed in the ILO Convention 169 (1989) and the United Nations Declaration on the Rights of Indigenous Peoples (UNDRIP) (UN General Assembly 2008). They have won emblematic legal battles at the Inter-American Court of Human Rights (IACHR), at times obliging states to recognize Indigenous territorial authority. In the decade-long case of *Sarayaku v. Ecuador*, the IACHR upheld the right of free, prior, and informed consent with a binding sentence against the Ecuadoran State for allowing a foreign oil company to encroach on ancestral lands without consultation during the 1990s. A 2011 petition by communities of the Xingú River basin led the IACHR to order Brazil's government to halt the construction of the Belo Monte Dam. The Mayan Q'eqchi' expanded jurisdiction by taking Hudbay Minerals to Court in Canada for crimes committed at an open-pit nickel mine in Guatemala. In Canada, two Manitoba First Nations used their own legal systems in 2013 to serve eviction notices to mining companies operating illegally on their land.[1]

International pressure is significant, yet states frequently eschew what they perceive to be uncomfortable mechanisms of accountability. Courts may validate Indigenous resistance, and UN reports warn against the catastrophic impact of extractive industries, but Brazil continued to build the Belo Monte Dam and Peru's government did not consider suspending the Camisea gas project of drilling 18 wells on protected territories that have been home to Amazonian peoples in voluntary isolation (Feather 2014). Nevertheless, states that evade prior consultation obligations only foster Indigenous inventiveness. In the absence of official mechanisms of consultation, people establish autonomous ones. Local communities of the Kimsacocha area took matters in their own hands after years of being ignored, demanding Ecuador's government consult them on a mining project in the highlands. In 2011, they organized a community-based consultation without the authorization of the state that was nevertheless legitimized by the presence of international observers (Guartambel 2012). The community voted 93% in favour of defending water rights and against mining in the area. Autonomous forms of prior consultation are increasingly common in Latin America. In Guatemala alone, there have been over sixty community-based consultations since 2005 (MacLeod and Pérez 2013).

Contesting States of Extraction

Indigenous resistance has been the target of severe government repression, ranging from judicial intimidation to assassinations of activists. Mobilizations against the Congo mine in Cajamarca, Peru, led President Ollanta Humala to declare a state of emergency and unleash military repression. An estimated 200 activists were killed in Peru between 2006 and 2011 for resisting extractivism (Zibechi 2013). Colombia's government, in turn, declared protests against the mining industry illegal. In Ecuador, about 200 people have been criminalized for contesting the corporatization of natural resources. Many have been charged with terrorism. Violent repression against TIPNIS protesters in Bolivia revealed that even Evo Morales, Latin America's first elected Indigenous president, is willing to use force to silence demands for consultation. Various activists opposing the multinational mining giant AngloGlod Ashanti have been assassinated. Argentina's Plurinational Indigenous Council, which calls for an end to extractivism, has recorded eleven assassinations since 2010. The Observatory of Mining Conflicts in Latin America (OCMAL) estimates there are currently 195 active conflicts due to large-scale mining. Peru and Chile lead the list with 34 and 33 conflicts respectively, followed by Mexico with 28, Argentina with 26, Brazil with 20, and Colombia with 12. Mega-mining alone affects nearly 300 communities, many of which are located on Indigenous territories.

This wave of intense criminalization indicates the expansion of the extractive frontier. In Peru, where anti-extractivist unrest toppled two cabinets under the Humala government and led to the militarization of several provinces, mineral exploration expenditures increased tenfold in a decade. In 2002, 7.5 million hectares of land had been granted to mining companies; by 2012 the figure jumped to almost 26 million hectares, or 20% of the country's land. Nearly 60% of the province of Apurímac has been granted to mining companies. In Colombia, about 40% of land is licensed to, or being solicited by, multinational companies for mineral and crude mining projects (Peace Brigades International 2011). According to OCMAL, 25% of the Chile's territory was under exploration or operation as of 2010. In 2013, Mexico's government opened the state-controlled energy sector to foreign investment, changing legislation to allow private multinationals to prospect for the country's oil and natural gas resources for the first time since 1938.

The problem is that governments are largely licensing Indigenous land. In 2010, the UN Permanent Forum on Indigenous Issues reported that Colombian mining concessions had been awarded in 80% of the country's legally recognized Indigenous territories. Colombia's government has 8.8 million hectares of Indigenous reserves designated as oil areas and granted 168 mining licenses on Indigenous reserves in 2011. Extractive industries lead to evictions, toxic waste, and resource scarcity, creating conflicts over water, soil, and subsoil. Open-pit mining uses unsustainable amounts of water. The controversial Marlin mine, partly funded by the World Bank in 2004, and today fully owned by Goldcorp, uses in one hour the water that a local family uses over 22 years (Van de Sandt 2009).[2] In Chile, mining consumes 37% of the electricity produced in the country – which will reach 50% in a few years – compared to 28% for industry and 16% for the residential sector. This requires the Chilean State to continually expand energy sources, thereby accelerating displacement and the transfer of agricultural land to hydroelectric projects.

Conflicts against extractivism should not be dismissed as only concerning Indigenous peoples. They encompass larger debates about the role of extractivism in politics and contest a development model based on the corporatization of natural resources. In particular, they reveal the continuous role of resource exploitation as a strategy to finance states. Governments are prioritizing extractive industries as key engines of growth, although there is ample evidence that extractive industries create relatively few jobs. President Juan Manuel Santos promised to turn Colombia into a mining powerhouse because it attracts quick investment. Opening Ecuador to mega-mining financed much of President Correa's third re-election. In fact, his unexpected policy shift to approve drilling within the Yasuní Reserve is explained largely by his government's urgent need for cash. China, which holds over 35% of Ecuador's foreign debt and financed 12% of its budget in 2013, buys about 60% of the country's oil and is expected to pre-buy Yasuní oil (Guevara 2013).

Indigenous claims against extractive projects contest a world system based on predation and usurpation. In Guatemala, mining is managed by long-standing political elites and inscribed in the colonial genealogy of power. In many instances, the entrepreneurs promoting mining today are the scions of the same oligarchical families that have controlled Indigenous land and peoples for centuries (Casaús 2007). The political economy of extractivism encompasses global inequalities of exploitation, within and among states. About 75% of the world's mining companies are registered in Canada, and most operate in the so-called Global South (Deneault et al. 2012). Extractive industries in the North rely on alliances with national elites to exploit natural resources of peoples and places historically marginalized from power politics.

Indigeneity as a Way to Rethink International Relations

Claims against extractivism are ultimately claims to the right of self-determination. The unilateral expropriation of land for mining today is a continuation of the Doctrine of Discovery. It conceptualized the New World as *terra nullis*, authorizing colonial powers to conquer and exploit land in the Americas. It also paved the way for a paradigm of domination that outlasted colonial times to evolve into a broader – and more resilient – self-arrogated right of intervention embodied by the modern state (Wallerstein 2006). Today, the idea of "empty" lands survives in extractivist practices. Large-scale mining by multinational corporations perpetuates the human abuse and resource appropriation initiated by Spanish colonizers centuries ago in the Bolivian mines of Potosi. International rights to self-determination may have replaced Papal Bulls, yet the political economy of looting natural resources on Indigenous lands continues, now in the name of development.

In this context, Indigeneity is a privileged site for the study of international relations. First and foremost, the extent and sophistication of Indigenous political praxis is relevant to any explanation of world politics. The rise of anti-extractivism as a politics of contestation against state exploitation calls for alternative sites of governance, such as the Inuit Circumpolar Council (Shadian 2013). Indigenous claims are shaping political practice, framing international legislation, and destabilizing assumptions about stateness. They seek the redistribution of rights as much as the uprooting of the concentration of power in the state. In that sense, Indigenous claims to consultation challenge the authority of states over natural resources as much as Westphalian forms of sovereignty.

Second, Indigeneity disrupts state sovereignty (Ryser 2012). The UNDRIP became the longest and most hotly debated human rights instrument in UN history because the expansion of Indigenous rights is intrinsically related to issues of state authority over territory. Rights to self-determination entail the recognition of plural forms of territorial authority in competition with states. Indigeneity is attributed to peoples who have historically been excluded from projects of state-making. Yet it contributes much more than making visible historically excluded groups. It refers to a politics that both precedes the state and lies outside of it. It is the constitutive "other" of the modern state, marked by a co-constitutive history that explains why Indigenous politics vary depending on different processes of state-formation. Consequently, Indigeneity is vital to a discipline dedicated to studying relations among states precisely because it is intrinsically related to state-formation. Standing outside of, and prior to, the state makes Indigenous standpoints valuable in terms of thinking critically about world politics and imagining what post-national political assemblages may look like (Sassen 2008).

Finally, Indigeneity is a strategic perspective in expanding scholarly debates on what *constitutes* IR. Indigenous experiences complement and broaden official national histories with forgotten or repressed narratives (O'Brien 2010), thus expanding methodological assumptions on how to do IR (Jackson 2010). Its precedence over the modern state encompasses alternative worldviews to think about the international beyond stateness. Indigeneity thus defies core epistemological foundations about power. In particular, it historicizes the state and sovereignty, moving away from Eurocentric conceptions of the world (Hobson 2012) and breaking with the discipline's unreflective tendencies (Tickner 2013). The vibrancy of Indigenous struggles not only confirms the inadequacy of the state, echoing calls to provincialize Europe's political legacies (Chakrabarty 2000), but it also provides concrete experiences of what the international can actually look like within and beyond the state (Tickner and Blaney 2013). Indigeneity is therefore doubly valuable for world politics. In addition to contributing alternative praxis of the international, it instigates critical theory to expand disciplinary borders.

Conclusion

Indigeneity is a valuable category of analysis for world politics. Indigenous experiences offer a fuller understanding of the world we live in. Integrating indigenous perspectives in the study of IR speaks to the ability to extend our political practice beyond the ivory tower. It is not a category of analysis that concerns merely Indigenous peoples, just as racism is not a matter for people of African descent only, or post-colonial studies the domain of previously colonized societies. The entire thrust of Indigeneity is that the non-state is the business of the state, and that there are alternative pathways available to decolonize the discipline.

Stripping IR of its state-centrism invites us to reflect upon the entrenched colonialism of international relations. Indigenous perspectives will hopefully inspire scholars to adventure beyond the conventional borders of the discipline. After all, opening an alternative locus of authority is nothing short of revolutionary.

References

Banerjee, S. (2012) *Arctic Voices: Resistance at the Tipping Point*. New York: Seven Stories Press.

Beier, J.M. (2009) *International Relations in Uncommon Places: Indigeneity, Cosmology, and the Limits of International Theory*. New York: Palgrave Macmillan.

Casaús, M. E. (2007) *Guatemala: Linaje y racismo*. Guatemala: F&G Editores.

Chakrabarty, D. (2008) *Provincializing Europe: Postcolonial Thought and Historical Difference*. Princeton: Princeton University Press.

Cott, D.L.V. (2008) *Radical democracy in the Andes*. Cambridge: Cambridge University Press.

Deneault, A., Denis, M. and Sacher, W. (2012) *Paradis sous terre: comment le Canada est devenu la plaque tournante de l'industrie minière mondiale*. Montréal: Écosociété.

Feather, C. (2014) *Violating rights and threatening lives: The Camisea gas project and indigenous peoples in voluntary isolation*. Moreton-in-Marsh, United Kingdom: Forest Peoples Programme.

Guartambel, C.P. (2012) *Agua u oro: Kimsacocha, la resistencia por el água*. Cuenca, Ecuador: Universidad Estatal de Cuenca.

Guevara, F. E. (2013, December 10) "La explotación del Yasuní: reprimarizacioón de la economía del Ecuador." *Opción- Ecuador*.

Hobson, J.M. (2012) *The Eurocentric Conception of World Politics: Western International Theory 1760-2010*. Cambridge: Cambridge University Press.

Jackson, P.T. (2010) *The Conduct of Inquiry in International Relations: Philosophy of Science and Its Implications for the Study of World Politics*. New York: Routledge.

MacLeod, M. and Pérez, C. (2013) *Tu'n Tklet Qnan Tx'otx', Q'ixkojalel, b'ix Tb'anil Qanq'ib'il, En defensa de la Madre Tierra, sentir lo que siente el otro, y el buen vivir. La lucha de Doña Crisanta contra Goldcorp*. México: CeActl.

Madrid, R.L. (2012) *The Rise of Ethnic Politics in Latin America*. Cambridge: Cambridge University Press.

Morgan, R. (2011) *Transforming Law and Institution: Indigenous Peoples, the United Nations and Human Rights*. Burlington, Vermont: Ashgate.

O'Brien, J.M. (2010) *Firsting and Lasting: Writing Indians Out of Existence in New England*. Minneapolis, Minnesota: University of Minnesota Press.

Peace Brigades International. (2011) "Mining in Colombia: At What Cost?" *Colombia Newsletter,* 18: 1–47.

Ryser, R.C. (2012) *Indigenous Nations and Modern States: The Political Emergence of Nations Challenging State Power*. New York: Routledge.

Sassen, S. (2008) *Territory, Authority, Rights: From Medieval to Global Assemblages*. Princeton: Princeton University Press.

Sawyer, S. and Gomez, E.T. (2012) *The Politics of Resource Extraction: Indigenous Peoples, Multinational Corporations and the State*. New York: Palgrave Macmillan.

Shadian, J.M. (2013) *The Politics of Arctic Sovereignty: Oil, Ice and Inuit Governance*. New York: Routledge.

Shaw, K. (2008) *Indigeneity and Political Theory: Sovereignty and the limits of the political*. New York: Routledge.

Tickner, A.B. (2013) "Core, periphery and (neo)imperialist International Relations." *European Journal of International Relations,* 19(3): 627–46.

Tickner, A.B. and Blaney, D.L. (2013) *Claiming the International*. New York: Routledge.

UN General Assembly. (2008) *United Nations Declaration on the Rights of Indigenous Peoples resolution / adopted by the General Assembly*. 2 October 2007, UN. Doc. A/ RES/61/295.

Van de Sandt, J. (2009*) Mining Conflicts and Indigenous Peoples in Guatemala*. The Hague: Cordaid.

Wallerstein, I.M. (2006) *European Universalism: The Rhetoric of Power*. New York: The New Press.

Zibechi, R. (2013, October 27) "Latin America Rejects the Extractive Model in the Streets." *Americas Program*. Available at: http://www.cipamericas.org/archives/10983 (Accessed 29 January 2014).

Endnotes

1. A delegation from the Red Sucker Lake First Nation descended on the work camp of Mega Precious Metals, Inc., a mineral exploration company, to stop them from working and demand that they vacate the land immediately. The Mathias Colomb First Nation issued a similar order to Hudbay Mining and Smelting Co., Ltd. and the Province of Manitoba.
2. According to the company's own social and environmental impact report, the Marlin mine consumes about 250 thousand liters of water every hour (MacLeod and Pérez 2013).

3

Self-Determination and Indigenous Health: Is There a Connection?

MICHAEL MURPHY
UNIVERSITY OF NORTHERN BRITISH COLUMBIA, CANADA

Self-determination is not only a *basic human right* to which all peoples are entitled as a basic requirement of justice, it is also a *basic human need* to which all peoples can lay claim as a fundamental component of their well-being. In other words, I am committed to the view that when their basic need for self-determination is met, peoples' lives generally will go better, and when it is not, their lives generally will go worse. To give substance to this view, I will engage in a cross-disciplinary exploration of the relationship between self-determination and indigenous health outcomes. More specifically, I will explore the hypothesis that meaningful self-determination in the form of greater individual and communal life control is a contributing factor to improved levels of indigenous physical and mental health, and, conversely, that control and domination by others is a contributing factor to ill-health and elevated levels of mortality in indigenous communities worldwide.

There are many different ways of defining self-determination, but perhaps the most useful in this context is in terms of the theory of human capabilities. To enjoy the capability for political self-determination is to enjoy a meaningful measure of control over one's political environment or a capacity "to participate effectively in political choices that govern one's life" (Nussbaum 2008: 605). To be freely self-determining in the political sense is part of what it means to be capable of living a free and fulfilling human life, and as such is partly constitutive of individual well-being (Sen 1999: 36–7; 2001: 11). Amartya Sen, the primary architect of the capabilities approach, puts it thusly: "Human beings live and interact in societies, and are, in fact, societal creatures. It is not surprising that they cannot fully flourish without participating in political and social affairs, and without being effectively involved in joint decision making" (Sen 2002: 79). While self-determination is most readily understood as an individual capability, my intention here is to focus on its significance as a collective capability, by which I mean a freedom whose nature "requires that it be sought in common" (Taylor 1994: 59).[1] Defined in these terms, self-determination is a capability that can only be realized in common by the members of a distinct political community, working together within shared political institutions to determine the laws and policies that will shape their individual and collective futures. The collective capability for self-determination encompasses the freedom to determine the character and boundaries of the political community itself, including the criteria for membership and political participation; the freedom to establish institutional mechanisms of collective deliberation and decision making that reflect one's own identity, language, and cultural norms; and perhaps most importantly of all, the freedom to make decisions that best reflect the values and priorities of the members of one's community in the absence of external interference or domination (Murphy 2014).

There is, in fact, a necessary interdependence between freedom as the capability for individual self-determination and freedom as the capability for collective self-determination, for it is simply illusory to speak of having meaningful control over the political decisions that govern our everyday lives within a political system imposed, by and largely, under the control of some external authority. Yet this is precisely the situation faced by most of the world's indigenous peoples, who have seen their collective capability for self-determination drastically restricted, if not effectively eliminated, as a consequence of colonization and modern state-building. The loss of self-determination has proven to be a source of intense frustration, anger, resentment, insecurity, and despair for indigenous peoples around the globe. It is also, in the eyes of many, one of the primary causal factors behind the tragic physical and mental health outcomes that plague indigenous communities virtually everywhere they are found, whether it be in the developing world or in the highly developed democracies of the modern West. How might these two phenomena be connected? What is it about the loss of self-determination that potentially leads to ill-health and premature mortality? One possible explanation is that indigenous communities that lack control, specifically over the administration and delivery of their own health services, enjoy poorer services leading to poorer health outcomes. There is some evidence to suggest that this is indeed the case, and that when indigenous peoples take greater control over health, this can lead both to better care and better health (Kalt 2008: 224–31; Dixon et al. 1998; Moore et al. 1990; Waldram et al. 2006: 276–8; Lavoie et al. 2010: 7). But is there something about the loss of political self-determination per se that is contributing to this ongoing health crisis? I believe there is, and recent research conducted in the fields of social epidemiology and social psychology helps us understand why this might indeed be the case.

I turn first to the research conducted by Michael Marmot and his colleagues on the social determinants of health inequalities. The first significant conclusion to emerge from this research is that inequalities in physical and mental health outcomes are strongly correlated with social and economic status. Specifically, people who enjoy higher social status generally have better health outcomes and people who enjoy lower social status generally have poorer health outcomes. The second key finding is that the explanatory link between health and status is autonomy: the degree of control people feel they have over their lives (Marmot 2004: 2). People with greater perceived control over their lives tend to be healthier, while those with lower perceived control tend to be less healthy. Lower perceived life control contributes to negative health outcomes both by influencing detrimental health behaviors (e.g. smoking, alcohol consumption, poor diet, physical inactivity) and through the production of chronic stress (Marmot and Bobak 2000: 133). The link between perceived control and health has been established in relation to a wide variety of health afflictions, including heart, lung and kidney disease, diabetes, mental illness, suicide, and deaths resulting from accidents and violence—the very same afflictions that are the leading causes of morbidity and mortality in indigenous communities worldwide (Marmot 2004: 6, 24; 2005: 1100–102). Marmot's research began with a focus on health in the workplace, but it has since expanded to cover a variety of different life domains and a variety of different interpersonal, social, economic, and political factors influencing health. In all of these domains, the conclusion that emerges is always the same: life control, or the capability "to lead the lives they most want to lead," is essential to people's health (Marmot 2004: 248).

A nearly identical message emerges from the research conducted by Richard Ryan and Edward Deci in the field of social psychology. Ryan and Deci are the originators of self-determination theory—an empirically derived theory of human development and well-being which identifies three basic psychological needs that "are universally required for humans to thrive" (Ryan and Sapp 2007: 75). First and foremost is the need for autonomy. To live autonomously is to live a life that is self-endorsed, a life that accords with one's genuine values and preferences. The opposite of autonomy is the feeling that one's life is being restricted, controlled, or dictated by forces that one does not freely or willingly endorse. The second is competence, which refers to our basic need to master certain skills or techniques that enable us to operate more effectively in the world and to achieve our desired ends in life. The third, relatedness, refers to our basic need for social connectedness, our need to feel a sense of belonging and a sense of importance to a larger social order or social grouping (Ryan and Sapp 2007: 75–6; Deci and Ryan 2012a). While each of these basic needs is essential to healthy development and psychological well-being, Ryan and Deci are unequivocal in their conclusion that none is more important than the need for autonomy (Ryan and Sapp

2007: 91). Self-determination theory has been empirically tested in a wide variety of social settings and environments, and these studies confirm that when any of these basic needs, especially the need for autonomy, is frustrated, psychological ill-health in the form of depression, anxiety, reduced self-esteem, feelings of hopelessness and passivity, and social dysfunction is the result (Ryan and Deci 2008; 2011).

The basic message that emerges from both of these research programs is that when people lack autonomy—when rather than feeling in control of their own lives, people instead feel that they are being controlled or dominated by others or by their social, economic, or political circumstances—their mental and physical health tends to deteriorate, and for those who feel the least autonomous, the outcomes are generally the worst (Marmot 2007: 1155–6; Ryan and Deci 2011: 59; Deci and Ryan 2012b: 85, 100–1). It should therefore come as no surprise that indigenous peoples, who are amongst the most socio-economically marginalized and politically disempowered peoples in the world, also have some of the worst health outcomes. And not only do indigenous people suffer from the same mental and physical ailments the foregoing theories would lead us to anticipate, they suffer, and die, from them disproportionately in comparison with the relatively more empowered non-indigenous populations with whom they co-exist (see, e.g. Marmot 2005: 1100–1). The ongoing denial of indigenous self-determination would therefore appear to be doubly destructive of indigenous health. It inflicts its damage, first of all, by eliciting feelings of anger, resentment, injustice, hopelessness, and despair that are the triggers for chronic stress and the negative health behaviors that prevail amongst those seeking to cope with chronic stress; and second of all, by maintaining indigenous peoples in a condition of domination and subordination, thereby denying them the most fundamentally important political means of satisfying their basic psychological need for autonomy.

In suggesting these conclusions, I maintain a healthy respect for the observation that sorting out the social and political determinants of health in any population is a very complex and uncertain undertaking, and that the available "evidence suggests that there is a range of factors at work, from the material to the psychosocial, and that it is difficult to assign ultimate primacy to any one" (Hertzman and Siddiqi 2009: 33). This observation is especially important in the context of the present discussion, given that systematic empirical studies of the relationship between self-determination and indigenous health are virtually non-existent.[2] Nevertheless, given the compelling relationship that exists between control and health in so many other domains of human life, it would be surprising if control in the political domain turned out to be entirely irrelevant. Indeed, given the overarching importance of collective self-determination in shaping the social, cultural, legal, and economic contexts that in turn help shape so many of the choices and decisions we make about how to live our lives, it would be even more surprising if it did not turn out to be of enormous relevance.

References

Chandler, M.J. and Lalonde, C.E. (1998) "Cultural Continuity as a Hedge Against Suicide in Canada's First Nations." *Transcultural Psychiatry*, 35(2): 193–219.

Deci, E.L., and Ryan, R.M. (2012a) "Self-determination theory." In: Van Lange, P.A.M., Kruglanski, A.W. and Higgins, E.T. eds. *Handbook of theories of social psychology: Volume 1*. Thousand Oaks, California: Sage Publications.

Deci, E. L., and Ryan, R. M. (2012b) "Motivation, Personality, And Development Within Embedded Social Contexts: An Overview Of Self-Determination Theory." In: Ryan, R.M. ed. *Oxford Handbook Of Human Motivation*. Oxford: Oxford University Press.

Dixon, M., Shelton, B.L., Roubideaux, Y., Mather, D., and Smith, C.M. (1998) *Tribal Perspectives on Indian Self-determination and Self-governance in Health Care Management*. Volume 1. Denver, Colorado: National Indian Health Board.

Hertzman, C. and Siddiqi, A. (2009) "Population Health and the Dynamics of Collective Development." In: Hall, P.A. and Lamont, M. eds. *Successful Societies. How Institutions and Culture Affect Health*. New York: Cambridge University Press.

Hunter, E., and Harvey, D. (2002) "Indigenous Suicide in Australia, New Zealand, Canada and the United States." *Emergency Medicine,* 14: 14–23.

Kalt, J.P., Henson, E.C., Taylor, J.B., Curtis, C.E.A., Cornell, S., Grant, K.W., Jorgensen, M.R., and Lee, A.J. (2008) *The State of the Native Nations: Conditions Under U.S. Policies of Self-Determination*. New York: Oxford University Press.

Kirmayer, L., Simpson, C. and Cargo, M. (2003) "Healing Traditions: Culture, Community and Mental Health Promotion with Canadian Aboriginal Peoples." *Australasian Psychiatry,* 11(1): S15–23.

Lavoie, J.G., Forget, E.L., Prakash, T., Dahl, M., Martens, P., and O'Neil, J.D. (2010) "Have Investments In On-Reserve Health Services And Initiatives Promoting Community Control Improved First Nations' Health In Manitoba?" *Social Science and Medicine*, 30: 1–8.

Marmot, M. (2004) *Status Syndrome: How Your Social Standing Directly Affects Your Health and Life*. London: Bloomsbury.

Marmot, M. (2005) "Social Determinants of Health Inequalities." *Lancet,* 365: 1099–104.

Marmot, M. and Bobak, M. (2000) "Psychosocial and Biological Mechanisms Behind the Recent Mortality Crisis in Central and Eastern Europe." In: Cornia, G.A. and Pannicià, R. eds. *The Mortality Crisis in Transitional Economies.* New York: Oxford University Press.

Moore, M., Forbes, H. and Henderson, L. (1990) "The Provision of Primary Health Services Under Band Control: The Montreal Lake Case." *Native Studies Review,* 6: 153–64.

Murphy, M. (2014) "Self-Determination as a Collective Capability: The Case of Indigenous Peoples." *Journal of Human Development and Capabilities.* DOI: 10.1080/19452829.2013.878320

Nussbaum, M. (2008) "Capabilities as Fundamental Entitlements: Sen and Social Justice." In: Brooks, T. ed. *The Global Justice Reader.* Oxford: Blackwell Publishing.

Ryan, R.M. and Sapp, A. R. (2007) "Basic Psychological Needs: A Self-Determination Theory Perspective on the Promotion of Wellness Across Development and Cultures." In: Gough, I. and McGregor, J.A. eds. *Wellbeing in Developing Countries. From Theory to Research.* New York: Cambridge University Press.

Ryan, R. M., and Deci, E. L. (2008) "Self-Determination Theory and the Role of Basic Psychological Needs in Personality and the Organization of Behavior." In: John, O.P. Robins, R.W. and Pervin, L.A. eds. *Handbook of Personality: Theory and Research,* New York and London: The Guilford Press.

Ryan, R. M., and Deci, E. L. (2011) "A Self-Determination Theory Perspective On Social, Institutional, Cultural, And Economic Supports For Autonomy And Their Importance For Well-Being." In: Chirkov, V.I., Ryan, R.M. and Sheldon, K.M. eds. *Human Autonomy In Cross-Cultural Context: Perspectives On The Psychology Of Agency, Freedom, And Well-Being.* Dordrecht: Springer.

Sen, A. (1999) *Development as Freedom.* New York: Knopf.

Sen, A. (2001) "Democracy as a Universal Value." In: Diamond, L. and Plattner, M.F. eds. *The Global Divergence Of Democracies.* Baltimore, Maryland: Johns Hopkins University Press.

Sen, A. (2002) "Response to Commentaries." *Studies in Comparative International Development,* 37(2): 78–86.

Taylor, C. (1994) *Multiculturalism. Examining the Politics of Recognition.* Princeton: Princeton University Press.

Tiessen, M., Taylor, D. and Kirmayer, L. (2009) "A key Individual-to-Community Link: The Impact of Perceived Collective Control on Aboriginal Youth Well-being." *Pimatisiwin: A Journal of Aboriginal and Indigenous Community Health,* 7(2): 241–67.

Waldram, J.B., Herring, D.A. and Young T.K. (2006) *Aboriginal Health in Canada. Second Edition.* Toronto: University of Toronto Press.

Endnotes

1.   The quote from Taylor actually refers to the idea of a "communal good," but it is equally apt in this context.

2.   Perhaps the closest thing we have to an exception here is the remarkable study conducted by Michael Chandler and Christopher Lalonde on suicide amongst indigenous communities in British Columbia, although they are inclined to interpret their results through the lens of cultural continuity. Be that as it may, the conclusion that emerged from this research is that indigenous communities which have secured a degree of self-government and local control over community services, and which are actively engaged in the defense of their territorial rights and the revitalization of their traditional cultures, experience low to non-existent rates of youth suicide, whereas communities which have achieved little progress in these areas experience drastically increased levels of youth suicide (Chandler and Lalonde 1998; cf. Hunter and Harvey 2002: 16; and, Kirmayer et al. 2003: S18 where greater emphasis is placed on community control as the underlying causal factor that explains Chandler and Lalonde's study results). In another study with important implications for the themes under discussion in this paper, Tiessen et al. (2009) find a correlation between greater perceived community control and improvements in the psychological well-being of individual community members, although they do not specifically link the concept of communal control to the idea of indigenous political self-determination.

4

Self-Determination as Self-Transformation

TIM ROWSE
UNIVERSITY OF WESTERN SYDNEY, AUSTRALIA

Let me begin with two propositions.

First, that Indigenous self-determination is both backward-looking and forward-looking; it is not only conservative and restorative, but also exploratory of progressive change. Self-determination necessitates a politics of cultural revision and adaptation in which Indigenous people cannot avoid debating among themselves what elements of their traditions they wish to preserve and what they would give up for the sake of adaptive innovation. Unavoidably, such debate among Indigenous people takes place in a context shaped by non-Indigenous political authorities and by global structures of economic opportunity and exploitation; self-determining Indigenous peoples have not chosen these contexts, nor can they ignore them.

Second, in each country where "Indigenous self-determination" is to be tried, its operational form will be determined by the geography and legal-political heritage of that country. Notwithstanding the discourse of global Indigenism (a useful discourse, but necessarily abstracted from place and time), there is no universal "Indigenous vision": aspirations are always emplaced and historically specific.

I want to illustrate these two propositions by telling a story about how Indigenous rights to land – surely a core feature of "self-determination" – have been configured in Australia.

Rights to land (and to sea) are both cherished by Indigenous peoples and problematic for them. In Australia, Indigenous landownership is extensive and increasing: in 2013, 0.715 million square kilometres was under native title (exclusive possession) and 0.682 million square kilometres was under native title (non-exclusive possession) – 18.2 per cent of the Australian land mass. The incidents of native title vary from land portion to land portion, and some titles fall short of the aspirations of the native titleholders. As well – and generally more satisfactory to the traditional owners – there are 0.981 million square kilometres (13 per cent of Australia) under various forms of "land rights." The Indigenous estate thus amounts to 31 per cent of the continent (2.379 million square kilometres), and it is growing because of a perpetual land acquisition fund (established in 1995) and because "native title" claims continue to be heard under statutory processes established in the 1990s. Indigenous Australians – at least, the minority of the Indigenous population living on these lands – are land-rich but income-poor. How does having such an estate contribute to their self-determination?

In Australia, there are no uncontentious answers to the post-colonial question: what should Indigenous people do with their territories (land and sea) once they have secured their rights to them?

That self-determination is a contentious process of innovation in land use is only implicit in the 2007 *United Nations Declaration on the Rights of Indigenous Peoples* due its understandable emphasis on preserving and defending what European imperialism has threatened to destroy (see UN General Assembly 2008). Because Indigenous people have been dispossessed, there are Articles about securing land and sea rights, to protect the Indigenous estate as lawful property. Thus, Article 8 of the *Declaration* says that "States shall provide effective mechanisms for prevention of, and redress" for "(b) Any action which has the aim or effect of dispossessing them of their lands, territories or resources." Article 10 says that "Indigenous peoples shall not be forcibly removed from their lands or territories." Other Articles intend to secure cultural traditions, and several times the *Declaration* uses the word "revitalize" when referring to such cultural continuity (see Articles 11(1) and 13(1), for example).

Can practices and beliefs be "revitalized" without changing them? A politics of innovation and adaptation are implicit in the preamble:

> *Convinced* that control by indigenous peoples over developments affecting them and their lands, territories and resources will enable them to maintain and strengthen their institutions, cultures and traditions, and to promote their development *in accordance with their aspirations and needs*.

The italics are mine: these words refer to phenomena that are not static, but dynamic. Indigenous "aspirations and needs" are in the process of historical formation. Here are some other examples of the open-ended nature of "self-determination." Article 21 says that

> Indigenous peoples have the right to maintain and develop their political, economic and social systems, to be secure in the enjoyment of their own means of subsistence and development, and to engage freely in all their traditional and other economic activities.

The phrase "other economic activities" points to a field of options that may not be "traditional." Article 22 says that

> Indigenous peoples have the right to special measures for the immediate, effective and continuing improvement of their economic and social conditions, including in the areas of employment, vocational training and retraining, housing, sanitation, health and social security.

Such "training and retraining" implies cultural change, most importantly the acquisition of literacy. Article 18 is a reminder that change is to be guided by the international human rights regime of which "indigenous rights" are a subset. That is, when empowered Indigenous people employ each other in their companies and other organisations, such relationships should be governed by norms (that may be new to them) "established under international labour law and national labour legislation."

Colonised people have always adapted – more or less successfully and under varying degrees of coercion. In this respect, the era of "Indigenous rights to self-determination" is continuous with the colonial past. The difference that "Indigenous rights" (such as those stated in the *Declaration*) can make is that Indigenous people may now innovate and adapt with more resources – material, legal, political, cultural – than were at their disposal when the colonising vision of their future was limited to exterminating them or assimilating them. One of the most important of these new resources – rights to territory – is also among the more potent provocations to change, to reconsider what "tradition" is worth. Land and sea, once secured, become "resources" in the service of new aspirations, and when Australian governments have recognised and granted rights to land and sea, they have positioned Indigenous Australians as subjects of self-transformation. In the rest of this article, I will compare the nineteenth century and twentieth century record.

Agriculture in the Temperate Zone

At first, land was conceded to Aborigines on the condition that they use it in certain ways that were new to them. In the earliest attempt by British authorities to reconstitute the Aboriginal relationship to land, the Lieutenant-Governor of New South Wales, Lachlan Macquarie, on 4 May 1816, made a peace gesture. He offered land tenure as an incentive for Aboriginal people to lay down their arms and to comply with colonial law. They would be granted land as long as they would develop it as farms, with government support in the form of six months food supply, agricultural tools, seed, and clothing. The only Aborigines who could enjoy such a benefit, Macquarie made clear, were those "really inclined and fully resolved to become a settler" (Watson 1914: 143–144). By contemporary standards, we could not characterise Macquarie's conditional concession of land as the British Crown's recognition of an Indigenous "right" to land. There is too much manipulation in Macquarie's policy; his ambition was "social engineering," prescribing a way of life that neutralised resistance to occupation.

However, other policies flowed from the view – found in some nineteenth century writings by British colonists – that Aboriginal tribes resided on land that was their collective "property" (Keen 2010).[1] While British-Australian legal doctrine explicitly set aside Aborigines' customary notions of property as irrelevant, the idea remained influential that it would be humane – an act of grace and conscience by the Crown – to limit dispossession.[2] Nineteenth century colonial authority, under the influence of this idea, came up with two devices that must be included in a history of Indigenous land rights: the conditional pastoral lease and the reserve.

To regulate colonial occupation, British authorities created a tenure known as the pastoral lease. Prompted by the Colonial Office in London, the New South Wales governor, in April 1850, proclaimed that pastoral leases could set limitations on the pastoralists' rights. The competing interests that the government had in mind were those of miners and Aborigines. The Colonial Office made its intentions to safeguard Aboriginal interests clearer when setting up land legislation in Western Australia in 1850 and in South Australia in 1850 and 1851. In the resulting stream of pastoral tenure law and policy, lessees were obliged to allow Aborigines to roam their properties, getting food and water as they had long done. The way that Aboriginal interests were imagined in this legislative tradition was prescriptive, but, in contrast with Macquarie's policy, it confined Aborigines to the pre-colonial past. They could access waters, animals, and plants on pastoral leases only in ways that continued their hunting and gathering traditions: they could kill a kangaroo, but not a sheep (leaseholder's property); they could harvest pre-colonial flora, but not the leaseholders' plantings.

In fact, the government's prescriptive power again proved weak. Aborigines residing on their ancestral country under pastoral lease-hold became a cheap labour force for the wool and beef industries, increasingly dependent on rations – later monetised as wages – and on welfare benefits, paid in kind or as cash. This adapted and exploited Aboriginal economy allowed many to maintain associations with their ancestral estates until the 1960s. In northern and central Australia, such pastoral coexistence was Aborigines' most significant adjustment to colonial authority.

The other nineteenth century device for limiting dispossession was the "reserve." From the colonists' point of view, it was an act of charity to set aside certain land portions for Aboriginal residents. However, historical research has recovered the agency of the Aborigines. Historian Heather Goodall has described an Aboriginal "land rights campaign" in New South Wales in the final quarter of the nineteenth century. In the 1870s, and up to 1884, twenty-nine Aboriginal reserves were created, and Aboriginal initiative can be found in twenty-five of them. By 1895, another eighty-five reserves had been created in New South Wales, and in forty-seven of them Goodall has traced Aboriginal initiative:

> Aborigines began to re-occupy their land. They "squatted" on small areas, built shelters, planted crops and then demanded that the government give them secure tenure... They wanted it, not just for economic reasons, but also to secure their access to areas that were within their traditional country... Aborigines were asking for full freehold and independent ownership, although they sometimes pointed out that they did not want the power to sell the land (Goodall 1988: 183).

Again, prescription accompanied recognition of an Aboriginal land interest. According to Goodall, these grantees "were told that the reserves would be secure as long as they continued to live there and farm the land" (Goodall 1988: 184). However, such prescription was, by now, less coercive and more aligned with the stated aspirations of Aborigines, for the colonised people in the southern agricultural zones of Australia were now presenting themselves as farmers. At Coranderrk (a Victorian government settlement established in 1861), Maloga (a Christian mission in New South Wales founded in 1874), and Poonindie (a farming community established in 1851 and managed by the Anglican church in South Australia until 1895), Aboriginal people were developing skills in agriculture and re-establishing their community and their attachment to land as people who sowed crops and managed herds – for themselves and sometimes as labourers for neighbouring colonists. While this change was made necessary, undoubtedly, by the collapse of their hunting and gathering economy in the face of colonial occupation of their land, we should not assume that this circumstance weakened their capacity to find self-respect and security in farming. Their petitions to government, when their aspirations were not met, proclaim their newfound identity as (what Macquarie had called) "settlers" – industrious, Christian, and aspiring to self-support.

For example, on 5 September 1881, the Coranderrk community compared their current manager (Mr. Strickland) unfavourably with his predecessor (Mr. Green). Mr Strickland "has no idea of tilling the ground or making any improvements on the station… We are all sure if we had Mr. Green back the station would self-support itself" (Attwood and Markus 1999: 46).[3] When the government legislated restrictions on who could reside at Coranderrk in 1886, the community's response linked their freedom of movement and residence with their participation in the region's market for agricultural labour. That is, they wished for "freedom to go away shearing and harvesting, and to come home when we wish, and also to go for the good of our health when we need it" (Attwood and Markus 1999: 50).[4] At around the same time, the Moira and Ulupna people, a few hundred kilometres to the north of Coranderrk, petitioned the Governor of New South Wales for land "to cultivate and raise stock." "We more confidently ask this favour of a grant of land," the petition continued, "as our fellow natives in other colonies have proved capable of supporting themselves where suitable land has been reserved for them" (Attwood and Markus 1999: 51).[5] At Poonindie, residents were dismayed in 1894-5 to hear that their land was to be subdivided as lots for unemployed colonists. Their petition asked for other land as a substitute: "we propose to live on it and cultivate and work the land among ourselves. With this and what we can earn by shearing fishing and getting guano, we can support ourselves and our families" (Attwood and Markus 1999: 55).[6] These late nineteenth century petitions from Aboriginal Australia make it clear that Aborigines who survived the frontier killings adapted, within a couple of generations, to the constraints and opportunities of the imposed economic order – if only colonial authority would encourage them with land security.[7]

Twentieth Century Gains and Losses in Remote Australia

Limitation of dispossession continued to be a strand of Australian colonial policy in the twentieth century. As the occupying authorities spread into the less arable interior zones (arid desert and lightly forested) and northern maritime zones (tropical savannah with pockets of rainforest), it proved more difficult to make money from these regions, as they yielded neither gold nor wool (the export staples that had enriched the six Colonies of Australia hitherto) in significant quantities. As well, humanitarian influence on policy had strengthened a determination to delay or prevent, in "remote" Australia, the catastrophic collapse of Indigenous economies and populations that had disgraced the British-Australian record in the southern, temperate, and arable regions where the immigrant population concentrated. Large tracts were conceded to Aborigines' continuing occupation, creating an enormous "reserve" estate, watched over by a light sprinkling of missionaries and officials. By the time global human rights norms produced the concept of tribal right to reserves (as in ILO Convention 107 1957), there was a large quantity of land whose significance to Indigenous futures was open to debate.

The putative Aboriginal estate at the end of the 1970s – when three jurisdictions had already legislated land rights and debate in others was raging – was 0.719 million square kilometres, or 9.3 per cent of the Australian land mass. Nearly all of that land was in remote regions, within four jurisdictions: the Northern Territory (0.382 million), Western Australia (0.220 million), South Australia (0.088 million), and Queensland (0.029 million). Most of these areas had been set aside as reserves in the forty years between the end of World War One and the late 1950s.[8]

It is important to note that the creation of this massive "welfare" estate was one of two major strands of twentieth century policy towards Aborigines. The other was the comprehensive inclusion of the Aboriginal population in a welfare system that guaranteed them supervised material sustenance (if they were not employed). Such provision was initially in kind – rations – but it was monetised between 1940 and 1975, as Aboriginal people were admitted, step-by-step, to full citizenship. Indigenous participants in the land rights debate had thus learned to value things in cash, and the prospective monetary value of once "worthless" reserve lands had increased as the continent had been mapped geologically. That miners now coveted the Indigenous estate provoked a politically effective mobilisation of the idea of land rights *against* mining, while awakening Indigenous perceptions of mining as an opportunity to escape poverty. The increasing immersion of Indigenous Australians in a culture of commercial valuation motivated, in part, their defence of the estate that had been conceded to them (Rowley 1972: 176). This perspective has not necessarily displaced their pre-colonial cosmology that links land and people in terms that the colonists recognised as "spiritual."

Sympathetic appraisal of Indigenous aspirations in the 1970s and 1980s captured this duality of Indigenous vision for their land. To offer but one example: "Almost all the Aboriginal submissions" received by Paul Seaman's 1984 inquiry into land rights in Western Australia, "reflect a strong anxiety to say whether or not granted land should be mined, but equally [they] do not oppose mining away from sacred sites, provided that its impact on their lives and lands can be controlled by them should they decide to permit exploration" (Seaman 1984: 38). Seaman appreciated that "Aboriginal people in nearly every part of the State are poor, that their organisations have pressing financial needs and that mining negotiations may be the only opportunity which they have to redress an almost complete lack of economic power" (Seaman 1984: 43).

Imagined Indigenous Futures

Thus, the imagined Indigenous futures have changed over the course of Australian history. In the land concessions of nineteenth century temperate Australia, they were expected either to participate in agriculture or to continue, somehow, hunting and gathering in the interstices of pastoral occupation; in the first half of the twentieth century, the benign vision was their indefinitely prolonged hunting and gathering in the remote regions, until Aborigines (somehow) gravitated to (some kind of) waged employment; in the period of "land rights" and "self-determination" (since the 1960s and in "remote" Australia), the most vigorously promoted Indigenous future has been some association with the mining industry: employment in it, licensing land to its use, for royalties, or even holding equity in it, for profit. Four other Indigenous "industries" have emerged (and whether and how each is compatible with mining is much debated): artistic production, for a domestic and global market; hosting tourists; land-management services to areas protected within Australia's vast terrestrial and marine "conservation estate"; and public administration. Some remote Indigenous Australians now participate in more than one of these.[9]

Recent changes in Australia's common law and statutes have vastly expanded the estate that grounds these five possible Indigenous economic adaptations. In June 1992, the High Court of Australia recognised "native title," ruling that it continued wherever lawful action by the state had not extinguished it.[10] A huge area of "unallocated Crown land" – mostly in Western Australia – suddenly became putative "native title" land. Governments, private resource corporations, and Indigenous leaders have spent the last twenty years adjusting their visions and behaviours to this radical remapping of Australian real estate, and I have summarised the quantitative results earlier in this article.

Native title and "land rights" are encoded in statutes that solicit more than one kind of Indigenous self-representation. One route to rights in land encourages "claimants" to prove their unmitigated fidelity to pre-contact culture: their economic adaptations count against them, as the descendants of the would-be farmers of late nineteenth-century Victoria and New South Wales (the Yorta Yorta) found to their immense disappointment in a definitive Native Title judgment and High Court sequel in 1998-2002.[11] However, in 1998, another route to economically rewarding land security was opened by amendments to the 1993 *Native Title Act* that empowered those asserting "native title" to negotiate with others who would use their land, without having to submit to the kinds of tests of authenticity that frustrated the Yorta Yorta. David Martin, a consultant anthropologist, argues that this second avenue is "part of a repertoire of social technologies which facilitate a move for the Indigenous people concerned to a more individuated and 'modernist' identity" (Martin 2012: 357-358).

Indigenous strategies of adaptation began the moment that colonial authority disturbed their way of life. "Self-determination" refers to a new phase of adaptation, in which Indigenous people demand (and hopefully get) new resources for self-transformation (more commonly known as "development"). What "development" "self-determination" will enable will vary according to the historical determinations and geographical features of the nation-states where it is attempted. After reviewing the successes and dilemmas of Indigenous mobilisation in the Americas, Karen Engle has warned of "the unpredictability of strategy – the inability of social movements ever to know that they are on the right long-term path – and the dangers of insisting that there is only one proper path" (Engle 2010: 274). Historical self-awareness of the paths taken in the past helps to minimise that danger, I suggest. When Australian governments awoke sufficiently to their colonial responsibilities to frame land rights and native title statutes that secured the large and growing Indigenous estate, they tended to recognise and legitimise the "spiritual" significance of "country" to Indigenous people, and Indigenous Australians certainly welcomed – as long overdue – this public affirmation of their ancestral culture as the basis of a pre-colonial sovereign right. In this respect they took part in a global trend in which Indigenous rights were framed, by Indigenous and non-Indigenous actors, as cultural rights. As Engle has argued, "increased cultural rights have sometimes lead [sic] to decreased opportunities for autonomy and development" (Engle 2010: 2). The question of culture is better posed, I have argued in this article, if we understand Indigenous self-determination as a self-transforming and open-ended project of political economy.

References

Altman, J. (2012) "Land rights and development in Australia: caring for, benefitting from, governing the indigenous estate." In: Ford, L. and Rowse, T. eds. *Between Indigenous and Settler Governance*. New York: Routledge.

Attwood, B. and Markus, A. eds. (1999) *The Struggle for Aboriginal Rights: A Documentary History*. Sydney: Allen and Unwin.

Barwick, D. (1972) "Coranderrk and Cumeroogunga: Pioneers and policy." In: Epstein,

T.S. and Penny, D.H. eds. *Opportunity and Response*. London: C. Hurst and Coy.

Engle, K. (2010) *The Elusive Promise of Indigenous Development: Rights, Culture, Strategy*. Durham, North Carolina: Duke University Press.

Goodall, H. (1988) "Cryin' out for Land Rights." In: Burgmann, V. and Lee, J. eds. *Staining the Wattle*. Sydney: Penguin/McPhee Gribble.

Keen, I. (2010) "The interpretation of Aboriginal 'property' on the Australian colonial frontier." In: Keen, I. ed. *Indigenous Participation in Australian economies: historical and anthropological perspectives*. Canberra: Australian National University ePress.

Langton, M. (2013) *The Quiet Revolution: Indigenous People and the Resources Boom*. Sydney: ABC Books.

Langton, M. and Webster, A. (2012) "The 'right to negotiate,' the resources industry, agreements and the *Native Title Act*." In: Bauman, T. and Glick, L. eds. *The limits of change: Mabo and native title twenty years on*. Canberra: Australian Institute of Aboriginal and Torres Strait Islander Studies.

Martin, D. (2012) "Alternative constructions of Indigenous identities in Australia's *Native Title Act*." In: Bauman, T. and Glick, L. eds. *The limits of change: Mabo and native title twenty years on*. Canberra: Australian Institute of Aboriginal and Torres Strait Islander Studies.

Peterson, N. ed. (1981) *Aboriginal Land Rights: A Handbook*. Canberra: Australian Institute of Aboriginal Studies.

Rowley, C.D. (1972) *The Remote Aborigines*. Sydney: Penguin Books.

Seaman, P. (1984) *Discussion Paper*. West Perth: Aboriginal Land Enquiry.

UN General Assembly (2008) United Nations Declaration on the Rights of Indigenous Peoples resolution / adopted by the General Assembly. 2 October 2007, UN. Doc. A/RES/61/295.

Watson, F. (1914) *Historical Records of Australia.* Series One. Volume 9. Sydney: The Library Committee of the Commonwealth Parliament.

Endnotes

1. As Keen points out, there were also observers, influenced by John Locke, who denied that the Aboriginal relationship to land could be called "owning," because these nomadic hunters and gatherers did not improve the land by mixing their labour with the soil.
2. That Aboriginal custom (at least in matters of proprietorship in land) is a source of Australian law was not recognised until 1992, when the High Court of Australia repudiated the doctrine "terra nullius" and proclaimed the concept "native title."
3. A petition was signed by fifteen named persons on 5 September.
4. As reported in the *Herald* (Melbourne) on 21 September 1886.

5. "Maloga Petition 1881," which had 42 signatories.

6. "Poonindie Petition 2 February 1894."

7. That the colonial governments of Victoria and New South Wales neglected this opportunity is the theme of Barwick (1972).

8. Peterson (1981: 2) defines "Aboriginal land" to include freehold, leasehold, reserves, and missions' portions.

9. For a celebration of mining's opportunities see Langton (2013) and Langton and Webster (2012). For a survey of the tensions among the options facing the owners of the Indigenous estate see Altman (2012).

10. *Mabo v. Queensland no.2* (1992) 1975 CLR 1.

11. *Members of the Yorta Yorta Aboriginal Community v. Victoria and Others* (2002) 214 CLR 422.

5

Knowledge, Technology, and the Pragmatic Dimensions of Self-Determination

MARISA ELENA DUARTE
PASCUA YAQUI/UNIVERSITY OF ILLINOIS, USA

Contemporary globalization depends on the ability of the elite to exercise a command over information and communication technologies (ICTs). ICTs include, but are not limited to, networked information systems, such as local and wide area networks, high-speed Internet, laptops, tablets, mobile phones, data centers, radio frequency identification systems, and increasingly sophisticated sensor-based and algorithmic surveillance systems. These systems of devices—and the people, policies, and institutions that support them—accumulate data and disseminate information for human decision-making across workplaces. When we consider how institutional leaders rely on commanding stores of advantageous information, we can perceive the nature of the information asymmetries that Indigenous peoples experience, rippling from the Enlightenment-era explorations of the New World to the intertwined government, military, and trade regimes comprising the cores of contemporary globalization. What does self-determination mean for Indigenous peoples whose daily work is shaped by connectivity within a global Internet superstructure and the trade value of indigenous knowledge (IK)? Where is the space for Indigenous self-determination within this networked environment?

As Indigenous thinkers, we must begin to understand the innovation of ICTs as semi-visible infrastructures growing within Indigenous homelands. Tracing the deployment of a fiber-optic Internet infrastructure across a sovereign homeland, such as the Navajo Nation, reveals an array of interlaced world-historical conditions, social and legal policies, and competing values orientations. From the romanticism of Silicon Valley to the hard rules of tribal sovereignty, these layers of meaning shape decisions about system design and deployment which, in turn, reveal the material and pragmatic aspects of

Indigenous self-determination (Duarte 2011; 2013a).

A remarkable example is found in K-Net, a multi-point wireless mesh network connecting First Nations communities in the lake lands of northern Ontario (Beaton 2009). As an outcome of their technical efforts, the network designers have become agenda-setters in local and national forums with regard to spectrum regulation, federal subsidies, tribal and industry partnerships, and Indigenous rights to Internet access. Their experience has shaped federal responses to First Nations technology needs and has inspired First Nations leaders to create a long-term broadband Internet plan (DeBruyn 2012). The growth of K-Net demonstrates the social shaping of large-scale technical networks and, specifically, an Indigenous example in which the values driving design decisions are grounded in Indigenous community needs and values.

Through examining various cases of Indigenous uses of ICTs, I have found that Indigenous peoples, in many different ways, harness ICTs to communicate more speedily with each other and with partners supporting tribal governance and grassroots social and political organizing (Alia 2010; Wilson and Stewart 2008; O'Carroll 2013; Woons 2013). Indigenous peoples who have a command over their local ICT infrastructure—through designing their own information systems to hosting tribal radio—are building a digital foundation for future practices of self-determination.

Social and Political Power and the Function of ICTs

How are exercises of social and political power shaped through the availability and accessibility of ICTs? A number of scholars have chimed in on this question (Mumford 1934; Ellul 1964; Heidegger 1977; Latour 1991; Law 1991; Star 1999; Tehranian 1999; Castells 2007; Wilson & Stewart 2008; Alia 2010; Howard 2010; Dourish and Bell 2011; Nahon and Helmsky 2013). The formulations that are most useful for understanding ICTs in Indigenous contexts are those that explain how elite classes of nationalist decision-makers utilize information gathered systematically through the media of ICTs to legally discriminate, economically exploit and disenfranchise, and otherwise subjugate Indigenous peoples in a continuous and cumulative fashion.

A prime example of this is represented in the history of the Cobell Settlement, in which banker and accountant Eloise Cobell (Blackfoot) accumulated years of data showing that the US government was not paying back to tribal landowners billions of dollars in revenues gained from the federal management of Indian trust land (Merjian 2010). Defendants argued that an accurate accounting was not technically possible, and yet through a painstaking audit, Cobell found the evidence of analog and digital systems rendering funds from the development of Indian land. These systems were not used to pay funds back—or even communicate an accurate accounting— to tribal landowners. This case reveals information asymmetry at work in Indian Country, in which systems of interlaced ICTs—including the hardware, software, policies, and administrators—are used to withhold actionable information from particular parties (Clarkson et al. 2007). One method of colonization is to articulate technical systems within elite institutions that withhold information, misinform, or disinform Indigenous peoples as a rule or practice. Indeed, Indigenous scholars have argued that Western universities are likewise designed to prevent the participation and deflect the theoretical interventions of Indigenous thinkers, specifically through habitually legitimating scanty and erroneous information about Native peoples as canonical knowledge (Dei 2000; Waziyatawin and Yellow Bird 2005).

Indigeneity Is a Phenomenon of Globalization

Thus, to understand the relationship between ICTs, Indigeneity, and self-determination, we have to understand the dynamic between inherently sovereign Indigenous peoples and the governmental classification of Indigenous bodies, lands, and forms of knowledge under a largely Western mode of globalization. We have to acknowledge how, when we think of restoring self-determination, we pursue a metaphor of Indigenous and Settler embattlement in which Indigenous ways of being are at stake within a milieu of homogenizing nation-state encroachment. There is an unvoiced periodization at play, referring to a perhaps false memory of a past era in which indigenous peoples enjoyed their own social organization, free of coercive governmental forces. We must unpack that metaphor and let go of the assumption that all Indigenous peoples bear the same land-based philosophy and attitude toward modernization within their homelands. The idea of capital-I global Indigeneity is fairly recent, and is best understood as an expression of the political solidarity that many land-based and nomadic peoples have in response to the exploitative aspects of nationalist pan-capitalist practices (Alfred and Corntassel 2009).

On the ground, in the communities, Indigenous peoples know themselves by the names and modes of governance they determined for themselves several thousands of years prior to the formation of modern nation-states. On the US Census, a Diné (Navajo) college student may report that he is a Native American. In addition to his Arizona state driver's license and US social security card, he may carry a tribal ID that proves his enrollment in the separate, sovereign Navajo Nation. He may use Facebook to encourage his friends to protest Mexican military violence in Chiapas and support Māori enforcement of the Treaty of Waitangi. But each of these political and legal expressions—Native American, Navajo Nation citizenship, Indigenous solidarity—fundamentally emerges from the Diné experience of the colonial US bid for sovereignty, subsequent nation-state bureaucratization, and current global military and economic leadership. Capital-I Indigeneity is a phenomenon of globalization (Niezen 2003). Capital-I Indigeneity allows the myriad of original non-Settler, non-nationalist peoples of the world to articulate politically with supra-national regimes, such as the United Nations and the World Intellectual Property Organization, while maintaining their inherently sovereign systems of governance, language, histories, and philosophies just out of reach of the commercial machinery of globalization.

Our young Diné college student could encounter a professor who challenges his Indigenous views. He could be stripped of his Navajo Nation membership due to internal challenges within the tribal political order. The US Census Bureau could eliminate the category of "Native American." Yet our student would still be Diné. The Diné way of being does not depend on the nation-state articulation or global economic order to exist. This is precisely why many nationalist regimes treat Indigenous expressions as a threat to the nation-state order. This is also the means through which we can begin to let go of the assumption that the political and social strength of Indigenous peoples is in the past. It is in the here and now, everyday, just under the gaze of the mass media Panopticon (Woons 2013).

ICTs and Indigenous Knowledge under Globalization

We can understand Indigeneity as a functioning part within the interlaced networks of systems, devices, people, policies, institutions, and terrains that comprise the technical ecology—the machinery—of militarized economic globalization. We can understand how Native ways of knowing become commodified within global markets. We can also understand how both physical access to ICTs and the values informing the use of ICTs—who gets to use these tools, learn to build them, toward what purpose, and how—shapes the ability a person has to participate politically and socially within the technical ecology underpinning globalization.

Above all, we can understand Indigeneity as a diffuse and flexible force of resistance to one of the primary political and economic mechanisms of globalization: colonization. Reaching back through the historical canon, we can identify many kinds of globalization—that is, governmental aligning of distinct economies toward cross-border trade while, at the same time, consolidating internal hegemonic order. Yet all of these, from the Silk Road through the League of Nations and on to NAFTA, cohere to at least three functions: they must enhance connectivity, profitability, and mobility.

We are at a point in the history of ubiquitous networked devices wherein the technical elite of computing languages is operationalizing toward a singular language, Internet Protocol Version 6. This technical solution allows for increased connectivity and mobility of devices. A Toshiba manager stationed in Ciudad Juarez can email AutoCAD files on her smartphone with the same efficiency as if she were in her Tokyo office. This supple and resilient mode of digital connectivity has encouraged what Bill Gates, Thomas Friedman, and others have deemed a frictionless form of commerce: cash and documents—paper—don't change hands, but rather numbers do across systems of devices (Gates 1995; 1999; Friedman 2005). Under a digitally networked mode of globalization, prices are fixed based on a knowledge theory of value, rather than through a pure market value. A coral and silver Navajo squash blossom necklace could, alternatively, be valued as a priceless gift from one family to another, purchased in Shiprock for less than a hundred American dollars, or sold online for ten times that amount in the Shibuya fashion corridor. The values of commodities are fixed based on what consumers perceive is their value within the range of the consumers'—not the manufacturers' or artisans'—experience.

It is within this digitized economic order that Indigenous peoples find their creative and spiritual expressions, medicinal and agricultural ways of knowing reduced to mere information and repackaged as IK within the supranational registry of intellectual property (Harry 2006; Smallacombe 2006; Belarde-Lewis 2011; 2013). Yet as Indigenous peoples know, the value of the squash blossom is not found on a fashion runway, but in the long histories and the homeland of the Diné people from wherein the design emerged. Here is where the values of an information-driven frictionless economy conflict with Native ways of knowing. The continual reduction of lived Indigenous experiences into bits within global trade circuits conflicts with the holism of Native ways of knowing.

Sensations of Globalization

Indigenous peoples' unique ways of being have emerged over millennia through the refinement of unique non-European languages, philosophical and spiritual orientations to the landscape, world-historical perspectives, and modes of self-governance (Holm et al. 2003). The expressions that emerge from this lived experience comprise whole ways of knowing. Salmon fishing comprises one Salish way of knowing. Drought farming represents one Hopi way of knowing. Silverwork comprises one Diné way of knowing. There are at least four mechanisms of colonization under globalization: classification of citizenry to subjugate Indigenous peoples; redistribution of lands and waters to nationalist settlers; articulation of institutions to enforce class rule and property ownership; and erasure of Indigenous languages, histories, and philosophies (Quijano 1992). When these mechanisms compromise Native ways of knowing, the ways of knowing gain a political significance, reflecting a set of values that in many ways paradigmatically opposes the centripetal force of globalization efforts.

For example, even if a Skokomish fisherman's particular technique for cultivating wild salmon can be scientifically shown to improve fish yields, reduce pollutants, and contribute to affordable local food stores, to patent that technique would, in one step, allow a single party to profit from this method while also preventing other peoples of the Pacific Northwest from utilizing that technique toward strengthening their own relationship with the living landscape. The subjugation of Native ways of knowing to intellectual property—Indigenous knowledge, traditional knowledge, or traditional environmental knowledge—and the subsequent commodification within global trade circuits exploits Indigenous peoples as peoples who are not recognized as sovereign governments by many other sovereign governments of the world.

The way of knowing becomes objectified, the part extracted from the whole, translated from a way of knowing to bits of data. The sensation for Indigenous peoples emerges physiologically. There is an association between the inability to grow or eat heritage foods and high rates of diabetes. There is an association between the inability to make a living through work that provides for tribal families and high rates of depressive behaviors. The violence regenerates, psychologically, emotionally, and spiritually. The ideation is of nationalist and capitalist encroachment through technical and economic means. Indigenous unwillingness to participate in industrialization of lands and waters, or reduce ways of knowing to the status of patentable technique or copyrightable product, has contributed to a widespread assumption that Indigenous peoples are anti-technological, which is only a paraphrase of prior colonial descriptions of Indigenous people as anti-modern, pre-modern, or pre-historic.

It isn't as if Indigenous peoples do not use and benefit from the availability of intellectual property rules, knowledge stores, and ICTs. A section of the UN Declaration on the Rights of Indigenous Peoples includes a reference to the right to affordable and robust Internet access for purposes of participation in self-governance. In the mid-2000s, when the regime of Canadian Prime Minister Harper initiated a series of bills abetting the removal of First Nations children from their families and erosion of homelands for an international oil pipeline, four Indigenous women utilized their programming and marketing acumen to launch the Idle No More social media campaign. The *Globe and Mail* reported that, from December 23rd to the 29th, 2012, the campaign went viral, generating between 19,000 and 25,000 tweets per day (Blevins 2012). Smart phones in hand, activists circulated invitations to flash mob prayer rallies and protests in shopping malls, public parks, and at select international borders from Albuquerque to Toronto. Checking Facebook and re-posting anti-colonial memes became an opportunity to transform a mundane technical activity into political empowerment (Duarte 2013b). This strikes at the core significance of what self-determination is: beyond an act of Congress, it bears a transformative capacity.

Pragmatic Dimensions of Self-determination

When, in 1978, the US Congress enacted the Indian Education and Self-Determination Act, it allowed American Indians to take command as tribes over their own social programs, free of federal supervision and intervention. A generation of Native people went to college, inhabited the world of Western ideas, combined those with Native ways of knowing, and transformed those into what are considered legitimate state-sanctioned forms of knowledge: books, movies, classroom lessons, school and health care programs. This represented a turning point in the histories of Native peoples within the US. Before, for at least three generations, a set of Spanish, French, British, and—later—Mexican, Canadian, and American nationalist social policies were aimed at erasing Native languages, histories, and philosophies and articulating institutions to destroy tribal modes of self-governance. For centuries, modern health care institutions, universities, banks, and courts relied on misinformation and disinformation about US Native peoples and their relationships with land and property, codifying these into false knowledge that pervades decisions to this day about tribal family dynamics, the psychology and spirituality of Native peoples, their scientific credibility and financial credit worthiness, not to mention treaty claims and rights to exist as separate sovereign peoples (Deloria and Lytle 1983).

At present, as Indigenous peoples, we are experiencing the articulation of information systems operating under a single computing language. Many of the systems we rely on everyday accumulate data that incrementally reifies the classification of Indigenous peoples as ethnic minorities; reserves lands and waters for future industrialization and human settlement; articulates institutions to enable elite nationalist class rule and commodification of property; and reduces Indigenous languages, histories, and philosophies to bits of information, devoid of the context of homelands.

This is precisely why, when Indigenous activists describe contemporary decolonization, it is spoken of in terms of restoring Native ways of knowing. To counteract the misclassification of Indigenous peoples, activists practice naming and claiming, and the enforcement of sovereign treaty rights. To counteract the settlement and industrialization of lands and waters, activists practice the sovereign protection of homelands and sacred places, ecological restoration, subsistence hunting, and tribal food practices. To balance the hegemony of Settler institutions, activists build Indigenous institutions, such as tribal colleges, clinics, and courts, as well as revitalizing sacred ceremonies, like the Bear Dance, and social ceremonies, like Canoe Journey. When Indigenous peoples speak original languages and share their histories and philosophies within the stream of contemporary world histories, they are able to relieve, locally, some of the more alienating sensations of pan-capitalist globalization.

Self-determination occurs the moment these practices become expected modes of community self-governance, as in the case of tribal courts. When we realize the ways that global information systems accumulate data for decision-making about Indigenous lands, waters, and bodies, then we can see how Indigenous peoples use information systems to build knowledge with one another toward self-determination. To design a tribal program takes information, including ways of knowing and the technical systems for channelling data, information, and knowledge. The Native Nations Institute at the University of Arizona is creating a database of hundreds of hours of videos of tribal leaders sharing their experiences. The Northwest Portland Indian Health Board hosts a database for recording incidence of disease across tribal communities, so that leaders can plan for their community's wellbeing. The work of Eloise Cobell represented a remarkable realization for many US Native peoples: we instinctively knew the land had been stolen, but an audit created the record to prove each case in a detail that could not be denied in US courts. Similarly, Idle No More represented a remarkable realization for many activists: here was a case that revealed the political capacity of Indigenous peoples communicating transnationally through social media networks and mobile devices.

Building the information systems—including the technical infrastructure, policies, interfaces, jobs, and educational programs—toward decolonizing Indigenous homelands is an act of self-determination. Sharing information inter-tribally, through networks of Indigenous peoples and allies, transforms silos of data into actionable information and builds communal knowledge about how to deal with the many manifestations of colonialism. For this reason, the Native American Broadband Association referred to broadband Internet across tribal homelands as the "third network," powerful enough to substantially change Native daily life. However, unlike the first two networks, the railroad and the electric power grid, US Native peoples can have a say over this build-out process (Native American Broadband Association 2011). Indeed, in 2013, the Navajo Nation completed a key phase in a $32 million dollar project to build a wireless mesh broadband network across the reservation, including a data broadband center and regulatory commission to oversee data flows, network use policies, and to strategize long-term planning. The goal is to create a digital environment in the Navajo Nation that makes it possible for the community to build their own systems for self-governance and the flourishing of Navajo language and culture.

Conclusion

Friedman ironically titled his 2005 bestseller *The World is Flat*. As Indigenous peoples, we are keenly aware that the world is neither flat nor frictionless. The sensations of immediacy, urgency, and placelessness that accompany heavy use of digital networked systems are also accompanied by sensations of alienation, information overload, and consumerist ideation. Indigenous peoples who observe the ecological devastation of their homelands due to economic wars of the global elite recognize the psychological and philosophical entanglements of a technologically dependent social order. But many Indigenous peoples also harness ICTs to surface Native ways of knowing that extend beyond situated locales. Designers of tribal community-based broadband Internet systems see their efforts as part of a bigger process for laying the groundwork to architect Indigenous possibility. Scholars and artists use ICTs to incrementally divest occupying powers in Native homelands across political, intellectual, and spiritual domains, filling the vacuum with ways of knowing that stem from an awareness of anti-colonial resistance and the hope for the flourishing of Indigenous peoples beyond colonialism. Indigenous uses of ICTs are about connecting to homelands, strengthening ways of knowing, participating in global markets as a matter of choice and not coercion, and disseminating Indigenous ideas about what it takes to survive, resist, and transform.

References

Alfred, T., and Corntassel, J. (2005) "Being Indigenous: Resurgences Against Contemporary Colonialism." *Government and Opposition,* 40(4): 597–614.

Alia, V. (2010) *The New Media Nation: Indigenous Peoples and Global Communication.* Oxford: Berghan.

Beaton, B. (2009) "Online Resources About Keewaytinook Okimakanak, the Kuhkenah Network (K-Net) and Associated Broadband Applications." *The Journal of Community Informatics,* 5(2).

Belarde-Lewis, M. (2011) "Sharing the Private in Public: Indigenous Cultural Property in Online Media." *Proceedings of the 2011 iConference,* University of Washington, Seattle, 8-11 February. New York: ACM.

Belarde-Lewis, M. (2013) *From Six Directions: Documenting and Protecting Zuni Knowledge in Multiple Environments.* Unpublished PhD Dissertation. University of Washington, Seattle.

Blevins, M. (2012) "The Hashtag Uprising: Analyzing #IdleNoMore's Social Media Footprint." *The Globe and Mail,* December 31. Available at: http://www.theglobeandmail.com/news/politics/the-hashtag-uprising-analyzing-idlenomores-social-media-footprint/article6825316/ (Accessed 31 January 2014).

Castells, M. (2007) *The Power of Identity: The Information Age: Economy, Society, and Culture.* vol. 2. New York: Wiley-Blackwell.

Clarkson, G., Trond, A., and Batcheller, A. (2007) "Information Asymmetry and Information Sharing." *Government Information Quarterly,* 24(4): 827–39.

DeBruyn, H. (2012) *The First Nations ISP Guide: Providing Internet Services, Managing Operations.* West Vancouver, British Columbia: First Nations Technology Council.

Dei, G. (2000) "Rethinking the Role of Indigenous Knowledges in the Academy." *International Journal of Inclusive Education,* 4(2): 111–32.

Deloria, V., Jr., and Lytle, C, (1983) *American Indians, American Justice.* Austin: University of Texas Press.

Dourish, P., and Bell, G. (2011) *Divining a Digital Future: Mess and Mythology in Ubiquitous Computing.* Cambridge: MIT Press.

Duarte, M.E. (2011) 'Resistance and Technology Roundtable: ICT4Sovereignty: History, Access, and Terrain in the Innovation of ICTs in Native America'. *Internet Research 12.0 – Performance and Participation (Annual Conference of the Association of Internet Researchers).* Seattle, Washington, 10-13 October.

Duarte, M. E. (2013a) *Network Sovereignty: Understanding the Social and Political Impacts of Tribal Broadband Infrastructures.* Unpublished PhD Dissertation. University of Washington, Seattle.

Duarte, M. E. (2013b) *Network Sovereignty: Building the Infrastructure Toward Intellectual Freedom in Indian Country.* Invited lecture at the School of Library and Information Science, University of Wisconsin-Madison, April 18.

Ellul, J. (1964) *The Technological Society.* New York: Knopf.

Friedman, T. (2005) *The World is Flat: A Brief History of the 21st Century.* New York: Farrar, Strauss, and Giroux.

Gates, B. (1995) *The Road Ahead.* New York: Viking Penguin.

Gates, B. (1999) *Business @ The Speed of Thought: Using a Digital Nervous System.* New York: Grand Central Publishing.

Harry, D. (2006) "The Rights of Indigenous Peoples to Permanent Sovereignty Over Genetic Resources and Associated Indigenous Knowledge." *Journal of Indigenous Policy,* 6: 28–43.

Heidegger, M. (1977) *The Question Concerning Technology.* New York: Harper Colophon.

Holm, T., Pearson, J.D., and Chavis, B. (2003) "Peoplehood: A Model for the Extension of Sovereignty in American Indian Studies." *Wicazo sa Review,* 18(1): 7–24.

Howard, P. (2010) *The Internet and Islam: The Digital Origins of Dictatorship and Democracy.* New York: Oxford University Press.

Latour, B. (1991) "Technology is Society Made Durable." In: Law, J. ed. *A Sociology of Monsters: Essays on Power, Technology, and Domination.* London: Routledge.

Law, J. (1991) "Power, Discretion, and Strategy." In: Law, J. ed. *A Sociology of Monsters: Essays on Power, Technology, and Domination.* London: Routledge.

Merjian, A.H. (2010) "An Unbroken Chain of Injustice: The Dawes Act, Native American Trust, and Cobell v. Salazar." *Gonzaga Law Review,* 46(3): 609–58.

Mumford, L. (1934) *Technics and Civilization.* Chicago: University of Chicago Press.

Nahon, K., and Helmsley, J. (2013) *Going Viral.* New York: Polity.

Native American Broadband Association. (2010) *Native American Broadband Association.* Available at: http://www.nativeamericanbroadband.org (Accessed 15 January 2014).

Niezen, R. (2003) *The Origins of Indigenism: Human Rights and the Politics of Identity.* Berkeley, California: University of California Press.

O'Carroll, A.D. (2013) *Kanohi Ti Ke Kanoha (Face to Face) – A Thing of the Past?: It's Cold Pressing Your Nose Against the Screen.* Invited lecture at the Information School, University of Washington, September 30.

Quijano, A. (1992) "Coloniality in Modernity/Rationality." In: Therborn, G. ed. *Globalizations and Modernities.* Stockholm: Forksningsradnamnden.

Smallacombe, S. (2006) "Think Global, Act Local: Protecting the Traditional Knowledge of Indigenous Peoples." *Journal of Indigenous Policy,* 6: 4–13.

Star, S. (1999) "The Ethnography of Infrastructure." *American Behavioral Scientist,* 43(3): 377–91.

Tehranian, M. (1999) *Global Communication and World Politics: Domination, Development, and Discourse.* Boulder, Colorado: Lynn-Reinhardt.

Waziyatawin, and Yellow Bird, M. (2005) *For Indigenous Eyes.* Santa Fe, New Mexico:

School of Advanced Research Press.

Wilson, P., and Stewart, M. (2008) *Global Indigenous Media: Cultures, Poetics, and Politics.* Durham, North Carolina: Duke University Press.

Woons, M. (2013) "The 'Idle No More' Movement and Global Indifference to Indigenous Nationalism." *AlterNative: An International Journal of Indigenous Peoples,* 9(2): 172–7.

6

Māori Self-determination and a Liberal Theory of Indigeneity

DOMINIC O'SULLIVAN
CHARLES STURT UNIVERSITY, AUSTRALIA

Māori and other indigenous scholars (Alfred 1999; Moreton-Robinson 2004; Maaka and Fleras 2005; Stewart-Harawira 2005) have well canvassed liberal democracy's tendency to affront the extant rights of indigeneity and constrain equitable indigenous political participation, even as both are admitted at international law (UN General Assembly 2008). Shaw proposes that the responsive politics of indigeneity is "an attempt to come to terms with how discourses and practices of sovereignty still set the conditions under which Indigenous – and other forms of 'marginal' politics occur at all" (Shaw 2008: 8). Indeed, Hobbes's account of sovereignty provides some understanding of why the democratic exclusion of indigenous peoples occurs:

> The structure of sovereignty that Hobbes produces is enabled and authorized through the production of a shared ontological ground, and identity. This identity, in turn, rests upon the necessary exclusion of Indigenous peoples at several different levels, not least through the explicit marking of Indigenous peoples as "different" as "Other". What is more crucial in determining the character of contemporary Indigenous politics, however, is that Hobbes renders the construction of this exclusionary identity, the process through which authority is produced and guaranteed, as pre-political, as necessary and natural rather than contingent and violent (Shaw 2008: 9).

Sovereignty reflects prevailing ideas about the sources, location, and nature of public power and authority, which means that its attendant discourses "are neither natural nor neutral. They reproduce a space for politics that is enabled by and rests upon the production, naturalisation and marginalisation of certain forms of difference" (Shaw 2008: 8).

The purpose here is not to diminish indigenous critiques of liberal practice, but to propose that rather than "move beyond the liberal paradigm" it may, in fact, be of greater pragmatic value to explore ways of broadening liberal democratic practice by advancing a liberal theory of indigeneity (Little 2003: 25). Such a theory would mean, at least, that one has the right to difference in cultural expression, but sameness in political opportunities; difference in forms of land tenure, but sameness in capacity to make decisions about how land will be used; difference in the way one is taught at school, but sameness in terms of educational quality. Indeed, a liberal theory of indigeneity constitutes a politics of distinctiveness, necessarily dependent on group rights – such as the rights to land, language, and culture – as inescapable constituents of individual liberty. Individual autonomy is contextualised, conditioned, and given substantive meaning and value with reference to culture and the inter-relationships that people, themselves, decide are important.

Indeed, there does remain scope for substantive "participatory parity" through a liberal theory of indigeneity that is beginning to replace biculturalism as the most influential political philosophy informing New Zealand Māori politics (Fraser 2003). Biculturalism assumed influence during the 1980s and proceeded on the assumption that the contemporary state comprised two distinct peoples, Māori and Pakeha (New Zealanders of European descent), living in a political partnership instituted by the Treaty of Waitangi in 1840. The Treaty saw Māori agree to the establishment of colonial government in return for the protection of their lands and resources and the rights and privileges of British subjects – the precursor to modern citizenship. However, the partnership developed as one where Pakeha effectively became the Crown, a term loosely used to mean the state, and senior partner to Māori, who were positioned beyond an inclusive sovereign polity (O'Sullivan 2007). Biculturalism did not protect Māori against the "tyranny of the majority" in ways that participatory parity proposes (Mill 1869). Participatory parity is concerned with the equitable distribution of the determinants of political authority and equitable opportunities for all people to deliberate in public decision making, for the citizen is, indeed, "he who deliberates" (Aristotle 1988). Public debate's importance "to the formation of values and priorities" makes participatory opportunities essential to people's sense of belonging to a political community that actually adds value to people's lives (Sen 1999: 153). It is also significant that

> In the absence of a Philosopher King who reads transcendent normative verities, the only ground for a claim that a policy or decision is just is that it has been arrived at by a public which has truly promoted the free expression of all (Young 1989: 263).

Participatory parity is a determinant of political capabilities, which are maximised when broader political arrangements bring "the people as close to good functioning as their natural circumstances permit" (Nussbaum 1987: 36). In other words, politics is "not simply the allotment of commodities, but [concerned with] making people able to function in certain human ways" (Nussbaum 1987: 1). This includes ways that flow from the enjoyment of the political conditions that allow *all* and not just *some* citizens to contribute to the determination of "the conditions under which and the practices through which authority is constituted and legitimated, and what these constitutions and legitimations enable and disable" (Shaw 2008: 1). It is in this context that a liberal theory of indigeneity requires ways of thinking about reclaiming the greatest possible political authority within the state, to confront prevailing prejudices and create opportunities to contextualize the meaning of individual liberty. A liberal theory of indigeneity grounded in the extant rights of first occupancy might attempt to re-shape public sovereignty to admit space for the culturally contextualized expression of common liberal democratic rights, as the first of a two-tiered differentiated citizenship (shared government), along with specific space for independent collective political authority as citizens of the tribal nation (iwi) – self-government. The second tier gives effect to the *Universal Declaration on the Rights of Indigenous Peoples'* recognition that the "right to lands, territories and natural resources is the basis for the collective survival and thus inextricably linked to their right to self-determination" (Daes 2008: 8).

Differentiated citizenship is a constituent of a liberal theory of indigeneity that is required to find

> A space within liberal democracies and liberal thought in which... Aboriginal perspectives and philosophies cannot only be heard, but given equal opportunity to shape (and reshape) the forms of power and government acting on them (Ivison 2002: 1).

The theoretical obstacles to thinking about indigenous politics in these ways are those proposing that there is no liberal democratic obligation to provide indigenous peoples with *particular* political recognition. Their capabilities are properly identical to those granted all citizens, and measures that transcend such a principle are illiberal privileges that affront the equal rights of other citizens. This is, as Kymilcka observes, culture's centrality to the claims of first occupancy creating a tension with the popular liberal perspective that "ethnic identity, like religion is something which people should be free to express in their private life, but which is not the concern of the state... it is not the place of public agencies to attach legal identities or disabilities to cultural membership or ethnic identity" (Kymlicka 1996: 4). Waldron's account of liberal obligations to indigenous peoples is similarly restrictive. It arises from his "supersession thesis," which holds that the entitlement to common, undifferentiated, liberal citizenship is sufficient to create just relationships capable of superseding historic injustices. Waldron associates the supersession thesis with a "principle of proximity," holding that people have a paramount duty to come to terms with, and to deal justly with, those with whom they are, in Kant's phrase, "unavoidably side by side in a given territory, irrespective of cultural or national affinity" (Waldron 2002: 30). However, if one is obliged to engage justly with all others, one must be attentive to the determinants of their political positioning in the present, because the present does not simply exist: it develops from history and is the product of political relationships and structures. If it is these relationships and structures, themselves, that are unjust because they are exclusive, one must consider their modification for inclusivity, and admit that the terms of inclusivity are necessarily culturally understood. The alternative, for minority indigenous populations, is that "belonging" to the liberal polity becomes "inextricably tied to white possession" (Moreton-Robinson 2003: 137) as the "definitive marker of citizenship" (Moreton-Robinson 2004: 79).

Nor can the inclusion of indigenous peoples in the sovereign whole occur under Waldron's proposition that "the general duty of a government to do justice to all people is [not] trumped by any special duty it owes to those of the inhabitants who can claim Indigenous descent" (Waldron 2002: 30). The equality that undifferentiated citizenship and liberal egalitarianism imagines is not the same as "substantive" political equality and stands well apart from the Rawlsian proposition that

> In the original position, the principles of justice are decided upon by free and equal citizens who do not know their own social status, class position, psychological tendencies, endowments of natural abilities or even their own beliefs about what is good (Hunter and Jordan 2009: 7).

Alternatively, the liberal order is equipped to admit theories of justice that codify the "duties of institutions and actors in reducing inequalities" (Ruger 2004: 1092), where a liberal theory of indigeneity would privilege particular measures to reduce political inequalities because "the goals of remedialism" must be transcended, not just "balanced" (Kowal 2008: 346).

Transcending the goals of remedialism might recognize group claims as an essential liberal concern, because group identity and experiences contextualize and shape the ways in which people experience liberty. The privileged group claims that Māori might then make are to a substantive share in national sovereignty that counters the assumption of the modern state as a Leviathan-like entity. Sovereign political authority might then be recognized as liberal indigeneity grounded in the claim that *all* and not just *some* people ought to share the "people's" sovereign authority.

The character of one's claim to a share in sovereign authority is an expression of the ways in which one prefers to "belong" to the political community so that sovereignty is inclusively "grounded in the right of all citizens to shape the society in which they live" by sharing in the setting of political agendas, priorities, obligations, and entitlements (Clarke 2006: 119). From this perspective, it is odd for the Māori party Member of Parliament, Te Ururoa Flavell, to have remarked that Māori ought to "get rid of the Crown's unconstrained sovereignty," because it is an argument that presumes Māori positioning beyond the Crown to set aside citizenship's first tier as the site of Māori participation as equals in the day to day affairs of the state (Flavell 2006). It positions Māori as interest groups, rather than peoples collectively entitled to certain rights of citizenship.

The Crown is not neutral, but nor is it the sole repository of the people's sovereignty. Its political authority is constrained and conditioned to create scope within the liberal paradigm for more inclusive and flexible understandings of political opportunities than that which Waldron proposes as the limits of indigenous entitlements (Waldron 2002). Flavell's ascription of sovereignty to the Crown from which he, as Māori, is distinct – even as he sought and was to become a member of the Government – makes irresolvable the perceived conflict between Crown sovereignty and Māori rangatiratanga, the term used in the Treaty of Waitangi to denote extant political authority exercised as chieftainship (Orange 1987).

Flavell's view can be rationalized according to a position that rangatiratanga constrains sovereignty. It is a common position that has distinguished conflicts between Māori and governments since the nineteenth century. However, one might alternatively understand rangatiratanga as providing a jurisprudential and practical liberal argument for Māori to claim both common and specific parts in a shared and dispersed national sovereignty, because rangatiratanga is always and inevitably exercised in relative and relational fashion to balance Māori interests against those of other citizens (O'Sullivan 2007). Rangatiratanga is not only legitimately part of the sovereign whole, but such positioning is necessarily preliminary to substantive self-determination *within* the state.

Rangatiratanga is also significant to the potential impact of citizenship's second tier, which is, for example, demonstrated through tribal commercial entities' increasing significance as economic and political actors (Nana 2012). Their significance among the sites of dispersed and evolving national sovereignty rises with their relative national economic importance. Their relative influence, as sites of public authority, increased with the devolution of public service delivery to iwi providers under new public management arrangements developed from the 1980s. Consumer "choice" in the receipt of primary health and other social services became marks of liberal freedom to complement the developing Māori education system's attention to Māori cultural and economic aspirations from Māori epistemological perspectives. These instances of liberal democratic choice give effect to a liberal theory of indigeneity's foundational assumption that "Māori should formulate policies for Māori and the role of the Crown should be to ensure that those policies were integrated into a workable state framework" (Durie 2003: 304). However, a liberal theory of indigeneity extends the aspiration to eliminate conceptions of the Crown as a distinct and exclusive non-Māori entity. Instead, there might emerge an inclusively constituted "people" from whom consent must be obtained for legitimate government (Locke 1887). Differentiated citizenship's first tier means, then, that Māori are necessarily positioned among the sovereign people in whose name the Crown governs. The best political arrangements are those that allow people to live "flourishing" lives (Aristotle 1998), which, among other considerations, depends on the distribution of sovereign authority according to principles of "objectiveness, reasonableness, necessity and proportionality" (Xanthaki 2008: 282).

Contemporary Māori politics reflects the beginnings of a liberal theory of indigeneity as an alternative to both biculturalism and undifferentiated liberal egalitarian citizenship as philosophical frameworks capable of providing Māori with a just share in national sovereignty, both as indigenous citizens and collectively through membership of the modern New Zealand state. Further development and practice of a liberal theory of indigeneity, through differentiated citizenship, is important to liberal democracy, which succeeds only when people have reason to share confidence in the system's capacity to distribute power and authority fairly, reasonably, and inclusively.

References

Alfred, T. (1999) *Peace, Power, Righteousness: An Indigenous Manifesto.* Oxford: Oxford University Press.

Aristotle. (1988) *The Politics.* Cambridge: Cambridge University Press.

Clarke, J. (2006) "Desegregating the Indigenous Rights Agenda." *Australian Journal of Legal Philosophy*, 31: 119–26.

Daes, E.-I.A. (2008) "An overview of the history of indigenous peoples: self-determination and the United Nations." *Cambridge Review of International Affairs,* 21(1): 7–26.

Durie, M. (2003) *Ngā Kaāhui Pou: Launching Māori Futures.* Wellington, New Zealand: Huia Publishers.

Flavell, T. (2006) *State of the Nation.* Available at: http://www.parliament.nz/mi-nz/pb/ debates/debates/speeches/48HansS_20060221_00000791/flavell-te-ururoa-debate-on-prime-minister%e2%80%99s-statement (Accessed 13 January 2014).

Fraser, N. (2003) "Introduction." In: Fraser, N. and Honneth, A. eds. *Redistribution or Recognition?: A Political-Philosophical Exchange.* New York: Verso Books.

Hunter, B. and Jordan, K. (2009) *Explaining Social Exclusion: Towards Social Inclusion for Indigenous Australians. Social Justice Discussion Paper No. 3.* Melbourne: The Social Justice Initiative.

Ivison, D. (2002) *Postcolonial Liberalism.* Cambridge: Cambridge University Press.

Kowal, E. (2008) "The Politics of the Gap: Indigenous Australians, Liberal Multiculturalism, and the End of the Self-Determination Era." *American Anthropologist,* 110(3): 338–48.

Kymlicka, W. (1996) *Multicultural Citizenship.* Oxford: Clarendon Press.

Little, A. (2003) "Multiculturalism, diversity and liberal egalitarianism in Northern Ireland." *Irish Political Studies,* 18(2): 23–39.

Locke, J. (1887) *Locke on Civil Government.* London: George Routledge and Sons.

Maaka, R. and Fleras, A. (2005). *The Politics of Indigeneity: Challenging the State in Canada and Aotearoa New Zealand.* Dunedin, New Zealand: University of Otago Press.

Mills, J.S. (1869). *On Liberty.* London: Longman, Roberts, and Green. Available at: http://www.bartleby.com/130/ (Accessed 13 January 2014).

Moreton-Robinson, A.M. (2003) "I still call Australia home: Indigenous belonging and place in white postcolonizing society." In; Ahmed, S. ed. *Uprootings/Regroundings: Questions of Home and Migration.* Oxford: Berg Publishers.

Moreton-Robinson, A.M. (2004) "The Possessive Logic of Patriarchal White Sovereignty: The High Court and the Yorta Yorta Decision." In: Riggs, D. ed. *Taking up the challenge: critical race and whiteness studies in a postcolonising nation.* Belair, Australia: Crawford House Publishing.

Nana, G. (2012) *Māori economy and wealth creation – Presentation to Auckland Council.* Available at: http://berl.co.nz/assets/Economic-Insights/Economic-

Development/Māori-Economy/GN-presentation-to-AC-and-IMSB-020812.pdf (Accessed 13 January 2014).

Nussbaum, M.C. (1987) *Nature, function, and capability: Aristotle on political distribution*. Helsinki: World Institute for Development Economics Research of the United Nations University.

Orange, C. (1987) *The Treaty of Waitangi*. Wellington, New Zealand: Allen and Unwin/ Port Nicholson Press.

O'Sullivan, D. (2007) *Beyond Biculturalism*. Wellington, New Zealand: Huia Publishers.

Ruger, J. (2004) "Ethics of the social determinants of health." *The Lancet*, 364:1092–7.

Sen, A. (1999) *Development as Freedom*. Oxford: Oxford University Press.

Shaw, K. (2008) *Indigeneity and political theory: sovereignty and the limits of the political*. London: Routledge.

Stewart-Harawira, M. (2005) *The New Imperial Order. Indigenous Responses to Globalization*. London: Zed Books.

UN General Assembly. (2008) *United Nations Declaration on the Rights of Indigenous Peoples resolution / adopted by the General Assembly.* 2 October 2007, UN. Doc. A/ RES/61/295.

Waldron, J. (2002) "Indigeneity? First Peoples and Last Occupancy." *2002 Quentin Baxter Memorial Lecture.* Victoria University of Wellington, 5 December.

Xanthaki, A. (2008) *Indigenous Rights and United Nations Standards*. Cambridge: Cambridge University Press.

Young, I.M. (1989) "Polity and group difference: a critique of the ideal of universal citizenship." *Ethics*, 99(2): 250–74.

7

Restoring Indigenous Self-Determination through Relational Autonomy and Transnational Mediation

RODERIC PITTY
UNIVERSITY OF WESTERN AUSTRALIA, AUSTRALIA

During the past decade, the right of Indigenous Peoples to self-determination has been substantially enhanced in international law, through the overwhelming endorsement by the UN General Assembly of the Declaration on the Rights of Indigenous Peoples. It is no limitation that this document is formally only a declaration, rather than a treaty itself, because it serves to illuminate the full scope of existing human rights treaties, in particular the two covenants on civil and political rights and on economic, social, and cultural rights, both of which begin by recognising that all peoples possess the right of self-determination. The character of contemporary international law has been clarified to include an Indigenous right to self-determination. This is a significant achievement, which was strongly resisted by many states while the text of the draft Declaration was debated and its endorsement delayed for over a decade until 2007.

The resistance of many states to restoring Indigenous self-determination as a right in international law was expressed in various ways, including a semantic refusal to refer explicitly to Indigenous Peoples In official UN deliberations. The annual gathering of Indigenous advocates at the UN is still called the Permanent Forum on Indigenous Issues, because states refused to acknowledge it as a forum for Indigenous Peoples, not just about them. When the forum was being created in 2000, Milelani Trask, an Indigenous leader from Hawai'i, affirmed in response to state intransigence that "We are peoples, not issues. Issues may go away, but peoples do not" (Niezen 2003: 164). She insisted that Indigenous Peoples be recognised as subjects of international law, with a capacity to exercise their right to self-determination, not merely as objects of decisions made about them by states. This capacity was not diminished by changes made to the draft Declaration before it was finalised, such as deleting a reference to the use of competent international bodies to resolve disputes between states and Indigenous Peoples regarding the interpretation of treaties between them.

Six years after the General Assembly endorsed the Declaration, it promotes a clear affirmation of the Indigenous right to self-determination that remains routinely denied in the practice of most states. The four states that opposed the Declaration in 2007 (Australia, New Zealand, Canada, and the USA) have belatedly supported it, but for these states, like for many others, endorsing the Declaration has been treated as a moral gesture requiring no substantive change to the state's political relationship with Indigenous Peoples. The political constraints on Indigenous self-determination have changed little since Kymlicka observed, in 1999, that Indigenous Peoples can obtain only "moral victories from international law," because "the real power remains vested in the hands of sovereign States, who can and do ignore international norms" (quoted in Xanthaki 2007: 119). Yet this situation of states dominating Indigenous Peoples and ignoring their rights is precisely what the Declaration was meant to help change. If the gap that Kymlicka highlighted between symbolic success and political neglect cannot be bridged, then Indigenous self-determination will not really be restored.

The main obstacle to restoring Indigenous self-determination is the refusal by states to renegotiate their political relationships with Indigenous Peoples based on the distinct status accorded to those peoples in the Declaration. As Xanthaki has emphasised, at the core of the Indigenous right to self-determination is the recognition of an Indigenous People's right to control their political destiny, to be included within a state on their own terms and through their own institutions (2007: 157-9). This right is essentially one of inclusive citizenship, which requires creating a relationship of non-domination between a state and the Indigenous Peoples living within that state. The Declaration provides a guide for how Indigenous self-determination could be restored, particularly in articles 18 and 19 about enabling Indigenous Peoples to participate through their representative institutions in all decision-making that concerns them. These articles support the principle of ensuring that Indigenous Peoples have relational autonomy from a state. As advocated by Young (2004), Xanthaki (2007), and Kingsbury (2000), this is the essential condition required for restoring Indigenous self-determination.

The principle of relational autonomy from a state, based on non-domination, has been contrasted by Young with the principle of non-interference or separation (2004: 189). Non-interference is unnecessary for genuine self-determination, both for Indigenous Peoples and for states. Yet the principle of non-domination is crucial for appreciating what is required to restore Indigenous self-determination. This can be outlined by reviewing how the refusal of states to help create new relationships with Indigenous Peoples is expressed at three different levels of complexity in their engagement with the UN, understood in the context of the three dimensions of UN activity highlighted by Weiss (2012: 8-9). These dimensions are, first, the basic structure of the UN as an international society comprising only states; second, the various agencies of the UN, which include bodies monitoring human rights treaties and the office of the UN Special Rapporteur on the Rights of Indigenous Peoples; and third, the broader range of transnational social movements engaged in advocating for both the member states of the UN and its various agencies to act cooperatively in support of the purposes of the UN Charter, including respect for human rights and self-determination of peoples. While these dimensions overlap, the main obstacle created by states is expressed at the level of international society. By starting with a review of the last two dimensions, it is possible to highlight the nature of the transnational transformation required to overcome the resistance by states to implementing the Declaration.

The collective engagement of Indigenous Peoples with the UN has been transformed in the past generation. Their plight was ignored by the UN for decades until the early 1980s, when they gained access to lobby a UN committee protecting minority rights (Coates 2004: 252). Although the process of creating the Declaration was difficult, once endorsed by the General Assembly, it gave Indigenous Peoples a status in the UN system superior to that of minorities within states who lack an Indigenous heritage. This was reflected in a recent call made by Indigenous leaders for the President of the General Assembly to ensure that an Indigenous representative works alongside a UN representative to facilitate consultations about the format of a UN Conference on Indigenous Peoples to be held in September 2014. These leaders claimed that, based on article 3 of the Declaration, Indigenous Peoples now have "the right of effective participation in all decisions affecting them" made at the UN (Littlechild et. al. 2014). When states face collective pressure from Indigenous Peoples asserting their decision-making capacity at the UN, it is hard for them to exclude Indigenous representatives from formal UN procedures. The fact that only four states opposed the Declaration in 2007 showed it is possible to shame states into supporting Indigenous self-determination at UN plenary meetings. In this context, states that support Indigenous rights are more likely to influence the positions of other states, by amplifying the voices of Indigenous representatives.

The fact those four recalcitrant states endorsed the Declaration by the end of 2010 was the result of much domestic lobbying, and the operation of a regular procedure for the UN Special Rapporteur, Professor James Anaya, to monitor the plight of Indigenous Peoples in particular countries. It is no coincidence that the first two of those four countries to renounce their opposition to the Declaration, Australia and New Zealand, were among the first seven countries investigated by Professor Anaya after he took over the role in 2008. Australia announced its support for the Declaration four months before Anaya's scheduled visit in August 2009, while New Zealand announced its support three months before Anaya visited that country in July 2010. For both countries, Anaya's reports (2010; 2011) were critical of entrenched discrimination against Indigenous Peoples, though his criticism would have been much stronger if the governments had not changed their policy to support the Declaration.

In Australia's case, Anaya's report amplified recent criticism by the Human Rights Committee of Australia for suspending the operation of legislation implementing the Convention on the Elimination of All Forms of Racial Discrimination. The Australian government initially rejected Anaya's criticism, but later modified its legislation after further criticism from the UN Committee on the Elimination of Racial Discrimination. While intense scrutiny from UN human rights agencies can lead governments to alter their policies, in this case only the form, not the substance, of the policy changed. The government ignored article 19 of the Declaration, which requires it to obtain the free, prior, and informed consent of Indigenous Peoples before adopting and implementing legislation or policies that affect them (Pitty and Smith 2011: 134). The government did not respect the principle of non-domination, despite responding to criticism from UN agencies about the manner in which it is perpetuating racial discrimination. While scrutiny from Anaya and other UN human rights agencies helped persuade Australia to endorse the Declaration and modify some legislation, it was insufficient to transform the government's lack of support for the Declaration in practice.

The main obstacle to restoring Indigenous self-determination is that governments face only occasional external pressure to uphold the principles of the Declaration. This is a substantial obstacle inherent in the dominant structure of the international society of states, which, as Bull argues, involves a "conspiracy of silence" between states about the human rights of their citizens (1977: 82). External pressure is needed to break this silence and expose the illegitimacy of state domination of Indigenous Peoples.

External pressure is a vital source of support for Indigenous Peoples, who, as Young notes, require regular and direct access to "agents outside the state" with "the authority and power" to influence how the state treats them (2004: 189). Yet, because of the conspiracy that Bull highlighted, only rarely will such agents be other states. While article 11 of the Convention on the

Elimination of All Forms of Racial Discrimination enables states to lodge complaints about breaches of this convention by other states, no state complained about Australia's suspension of its obligation to prohibit racial discrimination, nor highlighted this suspension to question Australia's credentials when it was elected as a member of the Security Council for 2013-14. Because of the conspiracy of silence, states still routinely tolerate the structural violence of racism in order to uphold the principle of not interfering in another state's internal politics.

If Indigenous Peoples lived in an external relationship only with international society, such as that which characterised colonialism, there would be little prospect of overcoming the political neglect of their rights by states that affirm the principle of non-interference. Yet the contemporary world is more interdependent and diverse than the colonial era. As Clark has observed, in recent decades "international society has been progressively encroached upon by global civil society," by various transnational social movements advocating for the creation of a world or cosmopolitan society in place of the inter-state order marked by the conspiracy of silence (2013: 35). Such advocacy, Clark points out, has often "been conducted through moral argument," which has helped to bring about normative change (2013: 35). The moral critique of the domination of Indigenous Peoples by states has established a basic premise for generating external pressure on states. This is the idea that the plight of Indigenous Peoples, in particular states, is now a matter of global concern. This idea is expressed in different ways through the UN, such as in the mandate of the Special Rapporteur and the holding of UN conferences. It is often expressed as a rejection of the Westphalian principle of non-interference. Thus, in John Pilger's recent film *Utopia*, Professor Jon Altman, an anthropologist at the Australian National University, says Australia requires international aid to help it transcend the powerlessness experienced in many Aboriginal communities.

This comment raises a vital question: what type of appropriate and feasible aid could help restore Indigenous self-determination in Australia? Because the problem is a political one, the aid must be of a type that could help overcome the political impasse that stops Australia from implementing articles 18 and 19 of the Declaration. Efforts to overcome this impasse within Australia have not succeeded. The need for Australia to facilitate a democratic process of recognising Aboriginal autonomy was highlighted 20 years ago by its most distinguished public servant, H.C. Coombs. He called for "an internationally recognised Act of self-determination" for Aborigines, but, despite the official apology in 2008 to generations of Aboriginal families forcibly separated by brutal paternalism, no such process has yet occurred (1994: 227). This shows there is a need for qualified international intermediaries to help Australia negotiate an Accord with Indigenous representatives, as advocated by the Aboriginal elder Mary Graham. She emphasised that independent, third-party negotiators, who recognise the legitimacy of each conflicting party, could encourage them to resolve their conflict (2001). Such intermediaries could help clarify the key terms of relational autonomy between Australia and its Indigenous Peoples, to be formalised in a treaty (Pitty 2006: 65).

Restoring Indigenous self-determination is a process that requires a dialogue between governments and Indigenous Peoples, in which both seek to create a new situation of relational autonomy, based on the core principle of non-domination expressed in the Declaration. The conditions for such dialogue are clearly stated in the Declaration, and repeatedly affirmed by the UN Special Rapporteur, by human rights agencies, and by transnational social movements. Where the prospect of dialogue seems distant, as in Australia, Indigenous Peoples are likely to seek external sources of support in their struggle for self-determination. It is likely that transnational mediation will be needed to persuade the Australian government of the need to recognise Aborigines' relational autonomy, based on the principle of non-domination. There is no guarantee that such mediation would succeed, but the growth of an interdependent, world society means that such international assistance could be both feasible and appropriate as a way of encouraging a shift from the idea of non-interference to that of non-domination.

References

Anaya, J. (2010) *Situation of Indigenous Peoples in Australia*. 1 June. UN Doc A/ / HRC/15/37/Add.4. Available at: http://unsr.jamesanaya.org/docs/countries/2010_report_australia_en.pdf (Accessed 29 January 2014).

Anaya, J. (2011) *The situation of Maori People in New Zealand*. 31 May. UN Doc A/ HRC/18/35/Add.4. Available at: http://unsr.jamesanaya.org/docs/countries/2011-report-newzealand-a-hrc-18-35-add4_en.pdf (Accessed 29 January 2014).

Bull, H. (1977) *The Anarchical Society*. London: Macmillan.

Coates, K.S. (2004) *A Global History of Indigenous Peoples: Struggle and Survival*. Houndmills, United Kingdom: Palgrave.

Clark, I. (2013) *The Vulnerable in International Society*. Oxford: Oxford University Press.

Coombs, H.C. (1994) *Aboriginal Autonomy*. Melbourne: Cambridge University Press.

Graham, M. (2001) "Application of the Oslo Model for Relations between States and Indigenous Peoples." *Landrights*. Woolloongabba, Australia: FAIRA Aboriginal Corporation. Available at: http://esvc000200.wic061u.server-web.com/lrq/

archives/200103/stories/oslo_model.html (Accessed 29 January 2014).

Kingsbury, B. (2000) "Reconstructing Self-Determination: A Relational Approach." In: Aikio, P. and Scheinin, M. eds. *Operationalizing the Right of Indigenous Peoples to Self-Determination*. Turku, Finland: Abo Akademi University.

Littlechild, W., Anaya, J., Aboubakrine, M.W., Choque, M.E., John, E. (2014) Letter to the President of the 68th session of the UN General Assembly. 16 January. Available at: http://www.un.org/esa/socdev/unpfii/documents/wc/letter-to-pga-3-mech-jan2014.pdf (Accessed 29 January 2014).

Niezen, R. (2003) *The Origins of Indigenism*. Berkeley, California: University of California Press.

Pitty, R. (2006) "The political aspects of creating a treaty." In: Read, P., Myers, G. and Reece, B. eds. *What Good Condition? Reflections on an Australian Aboriginal Treaty 1986-2006*. Canberra, Australia: ANU E-press. Available at: http://press.anu.edu.au/titles/aboriginal-history-monographs/wgc_citation/pdf-download/ (Accessed 29 January 2014).

Pitty, R. and Smith, S. (2011) "The Indigenous Challenge to Westphalian Sovereignty." *Australian Journal of Political Science,* 46(1): 121–39.

Weiss, T. (2012) *What's Wrong with the UN and How to Fix It*. 2nd ed. Cambridge: Polity Press.

Xanthaki, A. (2007) *Indigenous Rights and United Nations Standards*. Cambridge: Cambridge University Press.

Young, I.M. (2004) "Two Concepts of Self-Determination." In May, S., Modood, T., and Squires, J. eds. *Ethnicity, Nationalism and Minority Rights*. Cambridge: Cambridge University Press.

8

Implementing Indigenous Self-Determination: The Case of the Sámi in Norway

ELSE GRETE BRODERSTAD
UNIVERSITY OF TROMSØ, NORWAY

This article focuses on the issue of implementing principles of indigenous self-determination for the Sámi living in Norway. In order to capture core challenges related to implementation issues, the first section outlines the importance of adopting a relational approach to indigenous self-determination (see Kingsbury 2005; Young 2007; Murphy 2008). By using the explanatory power of this approach, it is possible to understand contemporary Sámi self-determination efforts in Norway. The second section connects the concept of rights to four stages of development of legal and political arrangements, which I present as a procedural outline for achieving Sámi self-determination.

A Relational Approach to Self-Determination

A relational approach helps capture core challenges related to implementing indigenous self-determination. Inspired by Williams (2005), it is useful to envisage two analytical normative spaces of political participation and governance. The first space is governed by indigenous peoples themselves through forms of autonomy and self-government. The second space encompasses the political system of the state as a whole. The perceived size and nature of the respective spaces vary and may depend on such factors as livelihood, cultural background, and territory (for instance, the Sámi could be either a minority or majority within a given region).

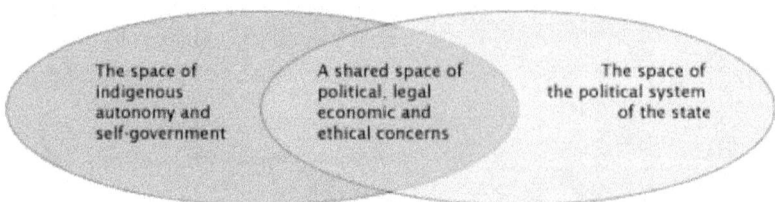

The space of indigenous autonomy and self-government | A shared space of political, legal economic and ethical concerns | The space of the political system of the state

At the intersection of these two spaces of political participation and governance are common political, legal, economic, and ethical concerns shared by indigenous and non-indigenous peoples alike (see above figure). This is the space where citizens, including Sámi citizens, must exercise their autonomy through participation in shared political processes. In this shared space, they articulate their interests, values, and rights by negotiating and debating issues of shared concern and issues of indigenous difference (e.g., land rights, cultural protection, and so on). Based on a deliberative and procedural understanding of politics aimed at achieving consensus in collective decision-making (Eriksen and Weigård 1999), the process of extending Sámi perspectives and participation into non-Sámi affairs can be described as the "integration of authority" (Broderstad 2008). A relational approach to self-determination captures and illuminates the potential of focusing on the integration of authority due to the approach's normative force in explaining complex interdependence between the policies, interests, and rights of indigenous and non-indigenous peoples.

In practical terms, a relational view of indigenous self-determination focuses on the ways in which the Sámi can extend political influence beyond the traditional domain of Sámi politics – beyond self-government in autonomous indigenous institutions – by incorporating their perspectives into mainstream decision-making bodies at local, regional, and national levels. As a result, indigenous peoples increase their influence though their increased ability to collaborate with the wider political community through closer relations with non-indigenous people. Equally important is the need on both sides to develop feelings of respect and trust. Building trust depends, in large part, on building political influence through autonomous indigenous institutions, like the Sámi Parliaments in Norway, Sweden, and Finland. The next section looks at some of the steps that can restore and maintain trust between the Sámi and non-Sámi.

Developing Legal and Political Arrangements in Four Stages

The development of Sámi rights over the past 30 years illustrates how political compromise and legal decisions further self-determination. On the one hand, courts (re)interpret evidence on important issues, like land rights, problematizing former understandings, policies, and approaches. For instance, the Selbu and Svartskog Supreme Court cases from 2001 both ruled in favour of the Sámi when disagreements arose over land use (Eriksen 2002; Ravna 2011). Such outcomes put pressure on the political system, which typically strives for compatibility between law and political practice. Particularly in common law contexts, Supreme Court decisions have played an important role in changing government policies on land claims. On the other hand, political solutions can be the driving force, modifying legal and political institutional arrangements. This was the case when the Norwegian Parliament adopted the Finnmark Act in 2005, which gave Sámi additional rights in Norway's northernmost county. Land disposition rights were conferred to a new landowning body, the Finnmark Estate (Finnmarkseiendommen), which administers land and natural resources in Finnmark on behalf of all inhabitants of the county. Prior to 2005, the Norwegian state considered itself the owner of 95% of the land in Finnmark, and this land was managed by a special state entity called Statskog. A political approach can draw attention to new ways of imagining the inter-subjective relationship between, and self-understanding of, both the Sámi and non-Sámi peoples. By making use of the political rights of citizenship, the Sámi have achieved significant breakthroughs in terms of their political influence and ability to self-govern. The following four stages help explain the path the Sámi have taken in Norway to increase their ability to self-determine, both in terms of increasing their autonomy and influence in the shared space of Norwegian politics.

Stage 1: The "Negative" Aspect of Rights and Political Participation

Like many other indigenous peoples around the world, the Sámi people of Northern Fennoscandia have a long-standing history of assimilation. The official policy of assimilation lasted roughly a century. However, unlike in Australia, Canada, and New Zealand, the Sámi were not historically excluded from voting in national elections (Murphy 2008). But like in Australia, Canada, and New Zealand, assimilation was gradually abandoned. The initial post-war period of sociopolitical development was marked by the need to recognize Sámi as equal members of the state, itself comprised of individual members, implying a uniform treatment of all without any recognition of cultural difference. This view was made clear when Norway ratified the International Covenant on Civil and Political Rights from 1966 without giving any relevance to the unique relationship with the Sámi (Minde 2003). Article 27 of the Covenant states that "In those states in which ethnic, religious or linguistic minorities exist, persons belonging to such minorities shall not be denied the right, in community with the other members of their group, to enjoy their own culture, to profess and practice their own religion, or to use their own language." A traditional reading of this article depicts rights as "passive" or "negative" rights preventing discrimination. It does not demand any active measures by nation-states. This did not change until the Alta struggle brought greater attention to Sámi issues and concerns, resulting in the Human Rights Committee – a body of independent experts that monitors the states' implementation of the conventions on human rights – which thoroughly examined the Norwegian position towards the Sámi in 1982-1983. The Alta struggle in the late 1970s is regarded as a turning point in terms of state policy towards the Sámi, which changed dramatically in the second half of the

1980s. The building of a hydroelectric power station on the Alta River bred conflict as Sámi protests and resistance efforts led to a dramatically greater sense of self-awareness and feelings of identity among the Sámi. Several dramatic events took place, including civil disobedience and hunger strikes outside the Norwegian Parliament. A strong alliance between the environmental and Sámi movements occurred, showing external support for their cause and leading to significant international attention on Norway's treatment of the Sámi.

Stage 2: The "Positive" Aspect of Rights and Political Participation

The second stage involves positively recognizing indigenous rights by calling on the state to honour the distinctive group character of indigenous peoples. Due to concessions made during the Alta affair, the Norwegian Government established the first Sámi Rights Commission (SRC) in 1980 with a mandate to propose solutions regarding Sámi rights to land and water, among other issues. The SRC argued for a new reading of Article 27, allowing for greater "positive" rights. The Norwegian Parliament followed this reading, implying that the nation-state had to actively contribute to developing Sámi culture, as well as embracing the material aspects of a minority culture. The authorities felt increasing pressure to be proactive on the subject. This is the stage when the Sámi institutionalization process made some headway. Based on the SRC's work, the Norwegian Parliament passed the Sámi Act in 1987, which led to the establishment of the Sámi Parliament in 1989. In 1988, a constitutional amendment (110a) was adopted, creating an obligation to secure and develop Sámi language, culture, and societal life. By securing and institutionalizing political rights through the Sámi Parliament, the Sámi became increasingly able to successfully argue for their rights, including the important issue of land rights.

Stage 3: The Procedural Aspect of Rights and Political Participation

The third stage is about enforcing procedural aspects that promote indigenous rights, which in the Sámi-Norwegian context have been implemented in the Finnmark Act in 2005 and the consultation agreement between the Norwegian Government and the Sámi Parliament that same year. The agreement regulates the relationship between the Norwegian Government and the Sámi Parliament. The consultation obligations of International Labour Organisation (ILO) Convention No. 169 on Indigenous and Tribal Peoples in Independent Countries are regarded as important premises for the agreement, designed to contribute to the implementation of the state's obligations to consult indigenous peoples under international law. In these processes, the interaction between national legislation and international law became particularly evident. The Finnmark Act has partly incorporated ILO Convention No. 169. The procedural aspects embrace the rights of indigenous peoples to consultation, negotiation, and real participation in decision-making processes. These processes are resulting in new arrangements for securing indigenous governance, and co-determination in fields such as the management of land and resources. In the past, the state has been able to ignore and even remove customary Sámi rights by overlooking rules and procedures found in internal law and principles of international human rights (Oskal 2001). Thus, in addition to public-judicial issues, procedures of clarifying customary land rights came into place. The evolving consultation practices seek to realize a partnership between the Sámi Parliament and state authorities. The enhanced recognition of rights expresses both a principle of autonomy and closer relations between the Sámi and the wider political community. The ability to build trust and political influence depend on the effectiveness of an autonomous Sámi Parliament to secure such arrangements. A representative political body had to be in place before the development of procedures of political inclusion could begin. Step by step, the Sámi Parliament has been empowered and stands out as the defining body in consultation processes with the Norwegian state. The Sámi have undoubtedly gained acknowledgement and the inclusion of Sámi concerns in a common legal framework is expanding, even if challenges and setbacks do sometimes occur.

Stage 4: The Institutional Aspect of Rights and Political Participation

Through consultation and negotiation procedures, indigenous institutions are empowered to deal with a wide range of policy matters critical for the implementation of indigenous self-determination. Thus, a fourth stage of enhanced institutionalization is taking place, entailing legal institutionalization. Institutionally anchored rights allow for extensive relations between autonomous indigenous institutions and state institutions. These relations require a complex framework outlining the jurisdictional powers of different authorities. Further, indigenous autonomy involves clearly defining relationships with state authorities, which implies constantly revising and politically justifying the framework (Kingsbury 2001). Illustrative of the increasing influence of the Sámi Parliament on relevant policy matters is the growing number of consultations with state authorities. Between 40 and 50 consultations on legislation and policies are carried out annually, with a majority leading to consensus. The topics are diverse, including consultations on education, health, language, national parks, cultural heritage, hunting and fishery regulations, reindeer husbandry, windmills, power stations, and mining. However, the number of consultations failing to reach agreement is also increasing. Still, the enhanced institutionalization and recognition of rights has made it possible to reach consensus and to move more firmly towards consensus through intermediate agreements requiring further steps or procedures for dispute resolution. The institutionalized consultation process promotes the involvement of the Sámi Parliament in state decision-making processes. The concerns defined within the space of self-government can be expanded upon and expressed more widely through the shared space of governance to the legislature. This being said, attention must be given to the fact that the opportunities for establishing indigenous autonomy differ. A unitary state like Norway primarily relies on transferring and delegating management tasks from central authorities to the Sámi Parliament. But there is gradual change in governance practices related to the Sámi as an indigenous minority. This is being accomplished through institutionalizing a consultation process – an exceptional case in Norwegian politics. Based on international law, on premises of real participation and influence carried out in good faith aiming at consensus or approval, the achievements of the Sámi Parliament are beyond those of just an advisory body. However, in practice this is not always so straightforward.

Having outlined these four stages as a roadmap for the recognition of indigenous rights, it is also important to note that setbacks in the struggle of Sámi rights recognition are apparent. A severe obstacle is the lack of recognition of historical fishery rights in coastal areas (Skogvang 2012). In 2008, the Coastal Fisheries Commission proposed to the Ministry of Fisheries and Coastal Affairs that all coastal residents had the right to fish in Finnmark's waters to maintain a reasonable livelihood. This conclusion was not accepted by the Ministry (Jentoft and Brattland 2011). Another contested issue is the new mining act (2009) where the Sámi Parliament and Norwegian Government failed to reach consensus. The government claims that the law safeguards Sámi interests, while the Sámi Parliament asserts the opposite, claiming that, among other things, the act breaches international law by not protecting Sámi rights south of Finnmark. These two cases on minerals and fisheries share one important commonality: they concern national resources with tremendous economic interests and political prestige. As is the case in the rest of the Arctic, politicians and industry leaders play a large role in how economic opportunities are developed. At the same time, this development may lead to greater conflict between industry, governments, environmentalists, and indigenous peoples. Governing systems handling conflicting interests – in this case, industrial activities versus traditional land use – must consider those who are most severely affected by exploitation activities and the duty of the state to protect human rights, including the rights of indigenous peoples against violations by third parties. According to Taylor (2013), this duty applies to all institutions of the state and involves standards of compliance for businesses to respect human rights, including government policy encouraging business to respect human rights. Without institutionally anchored rights and established procedures securing indigenous participation in state decision-making processes, the situation will only become more critical.

Summary

A relational perspective on implementing self-determination "encourages the view that indigenous peoples must seek influence in a variety of different political forums to manage the complex web of relationships in which they have become entangled with non-indigenous communities and governments" (Murphy 2008: 203). The relational approach makes the case that strengthening autonomy and self-determination through self-governing arrangements, versus extending indigenous perspectives and participation into non-indigenous affairs, are not necessarily contradictory. But the indigenous experience of seeking political influence and gaining self-governance is far from straightforward, as rights become necessary to counteract the arbitrariness of political decisions formulated through changing majorities in the state's democratic institutions. Political and legal reforms are needed for effective cooperation to come about by better managing the complex relationship between democracy and rights. The case of the Sámi in Norway elucidates one example of how indigenous rights can promote self-determination. The relational aspects of Sámi self-determination have evolved through four stages of progress: the "negative," the "positive," the procedural, and the institutional aspects of rights and political participation. The Sámi themselves have pushed the perception of rights into the public political consciousness by appealing to human rights standards and international law. Though the four stages are presented sequentially, the political reality is that various changes can deviate slightly. For instance, procedural and institutional aspects may appear concurrently. The point is that legal and political developments have made it possible for Norway's Sámi Parliament to directly influence state decision-making processes, which gives them a voice in a greater number of decisions affecting the Sámi. My emphasis on the relational aspects of Sámi political influence is not about impairing the importance of autonomy and the right to indigenous self-determination. On the contrary, I also claim that, in order to succeed with an expansion of authority, a relational approach to self-determination is required because the strengthening and empowerment of indigenous political participation depends on greater space for dialogue and shared understandings.

References

Broderstad, E.G. (2008) *The bridge-building role of political procedures. Indigenous rights and citizenship rights within and across the borders of the nation-state.* Unpublished PhD thesis. University of Tromsø.

Eriksen, E.O. and Weigård, J. (1999) *Kommunikativ handling og deliberativt demokrati. Jürgen Habermas' teori om politikk og samfunn.* Bergen, Norway: Fagboklaget.

Eriksen, G. (2002) "Tilvenningen til samisk kultur og rettstenkning i norsk høyesterettspraksis. Om møtet mellom en muntlig og en tekstbasert rettskultur." *KART OG PLAN*, 62(4): 228–45.

Jentoft, S. and Brattland, C. (2011) "Mot en samisk fiskeriforvaltning." In: Jentoft, S., Nergård, J.-I., and Røvik, K.A. eds. *Hvor går Nord-Norge? Tidsbilder fra en landsdel i forandring.* Stamsund, Norway: Orkana Akademisk.

Kingsbury, B. (2001) "Reconciling five competing conceptual structures of indigenous peoples' claims in international and comparative law." *Journal of International Law and Politics*, 34(1): 189–250.

Kingsbury, B. (2005) "Reconstructing Self-Determination: A Relational Approach." In: Aikio, P. and Scheinin, M. eds. *Operationalizing the Rights of Indigenous Peoples to Self-Determination.* Turku, Finland: Institute for Human Rights, Åbo Akademi University.

Minde, H. (2003) "Urfolksoffensiv, folkerettsfokus og styringskrise: Kampen for en ny samepolitikk 1960-1990." In: Bjerkli, B and Selle, P. eds. *Samer, makt og demokrati. Sametinget og den nye samiske offentligheten.* Oslo, Norway: Gyldendal Akademisk.

Murphy, M. (2008) "Representing indigenous self-determination." *University of Toronto Law Journal*, 58(2): 185–216.

Oskal, N. (2001) "Political Inclusion of the Saami as Indigenous People in Norway." *International Journal on Minority and Group Rights*, 8(3): 235–61.

Ravna, Ø. (2011) "The Process of Identifying Land Rights in parts of Northern Norway: Does the Finnmark Act Prescribe an Adequate Procedure within the National Law?" *Yearbook of Polar Law,* 3: 423–53.

Skogvang, S. F. (2012) *Retten til fiske i fjorder og kystnære farvann.* Unpublished PhD thesis. University of Tromsø.

Williams, M. (2005) "Sharing the River: Aboriginal Representation in Canadian Political Institutions." In: Thomsen, R.C. and Hale, N. eds. *Canadian Environments. Essays in Culture, Politics and History.* Brussels: Peter Lang Publishing.

Taylor, M. (2013) "Presentation on session III: Government regulation/framework for interaction between indigenous peoples and the industry." In: Broderstad, E.G. and Weines, J. eds. *Extractive industries and indigenous peoples.* Tromsø, Norway: Center for Sami Studies, University of Tromsø.

Young, I. M. (2007) *Global Challenges: War, Self-Determination and Responsibility for Justice.* Cambridge: Polity Press.

9

Revitalizing African Indigenous Ways of Knowing and Knowledge Production

HASSAN O. KAYA

UNIVERSITY OF KWAZULU-NATAL, SOUTH AFRICA

The article is based on the following arguments: the history of Africa's Indigenous ways of knowing and knowledge production did not begin with the coming of Western knowledge systems, and neither should their future depend exclusively on Western and other worldviews. Like other human societies across the globe, African indigenous societies have, for centuries, developed their own sets of experiences and explanations relating to the environments they live in (Kimwaga 2010). This is due to the fact that the way learning is perceived and how people actually learn is culturally specific. Different cultures have different ways and experiences of social reality and, hence, learning (Matike 2008). This is influenced by their worldview and belief systems of the natural environment, including the socio-economic and ecological context of their livelihood. These culturally and locally specific ways of knowing and knowledge production are often referred to as traditional, ecological, community, local knowledge systems, and so on. They encompass sophisticated arrays of information, understanding, and interpretation that guide interactions with the natural milieu: in agriculture and animal husbandry, hunting, fishing, natural resource management, conflict transformation, health, the naming and explanation of natural phenomena, and strategies to cope with fluctuating environments (Semali and Kincheloe 1999; Lander 2002; Kante 2004; Horsthemke 2004).

This article is based on experiences from a 2012 study conducted at Lokupung Village in South Africa's North-West Province. The study was conducted by Indigenous Knowledge Systems Programme students at North-West University, in collaboration with the North-West Provincial Department of Agriculture and Environment. The project was initiated by village community members based on their concern and experience with interfacing indigenous and modern knowledge systems. They indicated that, in most situations, the application of technologies from outside (such as extension services, hybrid seeds, fertilizers, chemicals, machinery, and credit systems) were not always appropriate to the local conditions, i.e. the local ecological conditions could be inappropriate for their applications, the inputs required might be unavailable locally, maintenance and follow-up systems might be lacking, or conditions might be socially or culturally (including linguistically) inappropriate.

In considering these factors, the following sections outline the challenges and prospects of interfacing African indigenous knowledge and other knowledge systems.

The Challenges and Prospects of Interfacing African Indigenous Knowledge and Other Knowledge Systems

The foundation of all knowledge systems is local, but due to unbalanced power relations stemming from colonialism and other forms of imperialism, other nations and cultures have universally imposed their knowledge systems, cultures, and languages (wa Thiong'o 1986; Timothy 1998; Schutte 1999; Walter 2002; Smith 2002). However, due to globalization, many problems – such as climate change, poverty, and environmental degradation – are global. This raises important question about how African Indigenous Knowledge Systems (AIKS) can contribute to the global knowledge economy. It is suggested that the sustainability of AIKS, given these global challenges, necessitates the convergence of African indigenous worldviews – embedded in African social practices through orality in their indigenous languages and knowledge systems – with other ways of knowing and knowledge production embedded through literality (Moodie 2003; McCarthy 2004).

In the context of this discussion on revitalizing African indigenous ways of knowing and knowledge production, the rationale for interfacing knowledge systems is twofold. It facilitates an intra- and intercultural dialogue between ways of knowing, knowledge production, and value systems. It also enables local African communities to better understand the differences and interactions between AIKS and other knowledge systems in order to reconstruct their own knowledge systems and to make better-informed decisions about which knowledge (internal or external) is appropriate for their sustainable future (Ntuli 1999; Seleti 2010).

A founding principle for fostering positive interactions between AIKS and other knowledge systems is that collaboration must be initiated between equal partners. It must be built on mutual respect and understanding, transparent and open dialogue, and informed consent and just returns for the Indigenous Knowledge holders and practitioners through the flow of rewards and benefits. While efforts should be made to combine the best of both AIKS and other knowledge systems, there is an increasing emphasis that intercultural learning should be based on local experiences as a necessary prerequisite and a first step towards intercultural dialogue of knowledge systems for the sustainable development of AIKS and its contribution to the global pool of knowledge (Odoro-Hoppers 2002; Lander 2002).

For example, in his discussion on the symbiosis between modern science and traditional knowledge for enhancing food security and climate change adaptation in Kenya, Mbuku (2013) looks at the use of indigenous knowledge in drought monitoring by pastrolists. He reveals that pastoralists usually derive Indigenous Knowledge-based forecasts just before the beginning of the farming season. He cites that, in northern Kenya, the Rendille pastoralists utilize a number of indicators – like local temperature, humidity, and wind conditions – to the presence or absence of certain types of clouds, rainfall patterns, and rain amounts. These weather indicators are also used in formal climate monitoring. When predicting prolonged drought, the Rendille pastoralists observe the flora and fauna for any unusual behaviour, paying specific attention to the noises made by certain bird species, the appearance of sparrow weavers, bees migrating, emaciated livestock species when there is plenty of pasture, the invasion of certain ants, the making of noise by crickets at night, and unusual flowering of certain trees (e.g. *Lonchocarpus sp. sterile*).

Astrological constellations, like the position of the sun and moon, are also observed in great detail by the Rendille and Gabra pastoralists. Speranza et al. (2009) show that a number of these indicators have also been used for drought monitoring in other communities, such as the Kamba pastoralists of Kenya. Nkondo (2012) states that, in spite of the various contentions on the effectiveness of the indicators used by indigenous communities around the world, Indigenous Knowledge Systems have increasingly attracted the attention of many observers in both developed and developing countries. Practitioners are starting to realize the importance of recognizing and working with Indigenous Knowledge Systems, which builds on generations of experience, to best support the adaptive capacity and strategies of rural communities (Orlove et al. 2010). There is increasing acknowledgement that indigenous forecasting methods are locally relevant and needs-driven, focus on the locality and timing of rains, and are "communicated in local languages and by local experts known and trusted by the people themselves."

Implications for African Educational Systems

The above discussion has implications on the current educational system in Africa – a system that remains predominantly Eurocentric and dominated by European worldviews. This is exemplified by the teaching of social sciences in African higher education institutions, where social theory is still entrenched in the methods, concerns, beliefs, and experiences of Western Europe and North America. Its irrelevance to Africa lies in the fact that it is quite inappropriate to attempt to fit African social history and social thought into the confines of a social and political structure that reflects the organisation of Europe 300 years ago (Schutte 1999). The implication is that African educational institutions, especially in higher education, have reduced themselves to the reproduction of the intellectual outputs of western social thinkers, including their theories and methodologies for prioritizing research. There is little attention given to African indigenous literary and philosophical traditions, as they tend to be viewed as primitive and unscientific, as well as improper sources for social theory and research development (Vilakazi 1999).

Nkondo (2012) reiterates the inability of African social scientists to generate their own indigenous concepts, definitions, theories, and methods which could guide the intellectual development in their research and academic fields. Smith (2002) adds that this leads to a lack of confidence among African scholars, as western research models, theories, and concepts are uncritically adopted and applied in African cultural communities characterised by poverty, rendering them irrelevant to local settings. They tend to be elitist because they focus on the concerns of dominant groups in society, which marginalises the views and concerns of underprivileged social groups.

The integration of AIKS into the educational system in Africa provides the following opportunities for learners and their respective societies: (i) It provides learners with the opportunity to learn appropriate community attitudes and values for sustainable livelihood. This is due to the fact that African indigenous communities have lived in harmony with their environment and utilised natural resources without impairing nature's capacity to regenerate them. AIKS in higher education can help to develop and promote these sensitive and caring values and attitudes for the environment. (ii) Learners will be able to learn through culture because AIKS are stored in various cultural forms – for example, folk stories, songs, folk drama, legends, proverbs, and myths. The use of these cultural resources in formal education can be very effective in bringing AIKS alive for students. It enables them to conceptualise, practically, the theoretical knowledge acquired in the classroom. (iii) Involving community knowledge holders in research, teaching, and learning enables learners to learn across generations, hence making them appreciate and respect the knowledge of elders and other community members. In this context, higher education will be an agency for transferring culture from one generation to the next.

Conclusion and Recommendations

While there are prospects in interfacing African Indigenous Knowledge with other knowledge systems, a generic application of foreign ways of knowing and knowledge production – including technology systems in African cultural conditions – is inappropriate. Knowledge systems should build on locally available resources, primarily the cultural and environmental experiences of the local people for relevance and sustainability. This has implications for African educational systems and sustainable community development: the necessity for direct collaboration between local communities and institutions of learning at all levels; intra- and inter-cultural education and research, which should be a collaborative effort of institutions of learning and local communities; and the dialogue and interface of ways of knowing and knowledge production, which can play an important role in re-indigenisation of educational systems in Africa. This will facilitate an intra- and intercultural dialogue between knowledge systems. However, this process requires reforming the education system in general to accommodate the new paradigm in ways of knowing, knowledge production, and value systems.

References

Horsthemke, K. (2004) "'Indigenous Knowledge' – Conceptions and Misconceptions." *Journal of Education,* 32: 1–15.

Kante, P. (2004) "Indigenous Knowledge and Environmental Concerns in Africa." *Economic and Political Weekly,* 4(22): 31–44.

Kimwaga, S. (2010) *African Indigenous Psychology and Eurocentrism.* Unpublished Manuscript. Dar es Salaam, Tanzania: College of Business Education.

Lander, D. (2002) "Eurocentrism and Colonialism in Africa." *Nepantla,* 1(2): 510–32.

Matike, E. (2008) *Knowledge and Perceptions of Educators and Learners in the Incorporation of IKS into School Curriculum.* Unpublished BA (Honours) thesis. North-West University, South Africa.

Mbuku, S.M. (2013) "The Symbiosis Between Modern Science And Traditional Knowledge For Enhancing Food Security And Climate Change Adaptation in Kenya." In: United Nations Conference On Trade And Development, *Trade and Environment Review (2013). Wake Up Before It is Too Late. Make Agriculture Truly Sustainable for Food Security in a Changing Climate.* Geneva.

McCarthy, S. (2004) "Globalization and Education." In: William, B. ed. *The Book of Virtues.* New York: Simon and Schuster.

Moodie, T. (2003) "Alternative Ways of Knowing – Doing Justice to Non-Western Intellectual Traditions in A Postmodern Era." *Journal of Education (Kenton Special Edition),* 31: 7–24.

Nkondo, M. (2012) "Indigenous African Knowledge Systems In A Polyepistemic World: The Capabilities Approach And The Translatability Of Knowledge Systems." *The Southern African Regional Colloquium On Indigenous African Knowledge Systems: Methodologies And Epistemologies For Research, Teaching, Learning And Community Engagement In Higher Education.* University Of Kwazulu-Natal 23 November 2012. Howard College.

Ntuli, P. (1999) "The Missing Link Between Culture And Education: Are We Still Chasing Gods That Are Not Our Own?" In: Makgoba, M.W. ed. *African Renaissance.* Cape Town, South Africa: Mafube-Tafelberg.

Odora-Hoppers, C.A. ed. (2002) *Indigenous Knowledge and the Integration of Knowledge Systems: Towards a Philosophy of Articulation.* Claremont, South Africa: New Africa Books.

Orlove, B., Roncoli C., Kabugo, M. and Majugu, A. (2010) "Indigenous climate knowledge in southern Uganda: The multiple components of a dynamic regional system." *Climate Change,* 100: 243–65.

Schutte, G. (1999) "Colonialism and Eurocentrism." *Review of Anthropology,* 22(2): 120–34.

Seleti, Y.N. (2010) "Interfacing Indigenous Knowledge with Other Knowledge Systems in the Knowledge Economy: The South African Case." *Library Symposium 2010: Presidential Meeting. Knowing is not enough: Engaging in the knowledge economy.* Stellenbosch University 18-19 February 2010.

Semali, L.M. and Kincheloe, J. L. (1999) "Introduction: What is Indigenous Knowledge and Why Should We Study It?" In: Semali, L.M. and Kincheloe, J.L. eds. *What is Indigenous Knowledge? Voices from the Academy.* New York and London: Falmer Press.

Smith, A. (2002) "Power and Hierarchy of Knowledge." *Geoforum,* 40(1): 230–48.

Speranza C.I., Kiteme B., Ambenje P., Wiesmann, U. and Makali, S. (2009) "Indigenous Knowledge Related To Climate Variability And Change: Insights From Droughts In Semi-Arid Areas Of Former Makueni District, Kenya." *Climate Change,* 100: 295–315.

Timothy, R. (1998) "Views from the South: Intellectual Hegemony and Postmodernism in Developing Societies." *Review of Anthropology,* 20(1): 61–78.

Vilakazi, H.W. (1999) "The Problem of African Universities." In: Makgoba M.W. ed. *African Renaissance.* Cape Town, South Africa: Mafube-Tafelberg.

wa Thiong'o, N. (1986) *Decolonizing the Mind: The Politics of Language in African Literature.* Nairobi, Kenya: Heinemann.

Walter, D. (2002) "Colonial and Post-Colonial Discourses in Social Sciences: A Cultural Critique of Colonialism." *Latin American Research Review,* 28(3): 120–34.

10

China and the UN Declaration on the Rights of Indigenous Peoples: The Case of Tibet

MICHAEL DAVIS

UNIVERSITY OF HONG KONG, HONG KONG

Using sovereignty as a shield, the People's Republic of China (PRC) has generally sought a pass in regard to enforcing international human rights compliance. Though it has signed numerous human rights treaties, its state-centered approach has sought to avoid all efforts at enforcement. This avoidance has nowhere been more absolute than its disavowal of any obligations regarding indigenous peoples' rights. The PRC actually voted in support of the 2007 United Nations Declaration on the Rights of Indigenous Peoples (UNDRIP) (UN General Assembly 2008). It then promptly disavowed any obligation under the declaration, proclaiming there were no indigenous peoples in China. It proclaimed 5,000 years of unity and harmony with its 55 designated national minorities living in peace on their own land. Though a bloody history and recent protests by the most prominent of these minorities – Tibetans, Uyghurs, and Mongols – would tend to belie such assertion, the international community has rarely challenged this claim.

PRC protestations aside, a reasonable case can be made that China does have indigenous peoples among the peoples it has formally identified as national minorities. Narrowing the focus to Tibet, this article will assess China's claims of exception from indigenous obligations and evaluate, on a general level, compliance with relevant international standards. This analysis appreciates that a mere UN declaration is usually not considered hard international law, though it may, under some circumstances, reflect customary international law. At a minimum, the UNDRIP, which sought to reflect existing customary international law, may be judged to offer a compelling guideline that China itself effectively embraced with its supporting vote.

The UN Declaration and China

While the UNDRIP does not offer a specific definition of "indigenous peoples," it does specify that they exist throughout the world.[1] A 1986 UN study offered a definition seeking to include "communities... which, having a historical continuity with pre-invasion and pre-colonial societies that developed on their territories, consider themselves distinct from other sectors of the societies now prevailing" (UN Economic and Social Council 1986). The emphasis on distinctive self-identification clearly applies in this case. Even by China's own account, in its 2009 White Paper on Tibet, the Tibetan people are clearly recognized as having a distinctive culture, language, and history, and constitute the vast majority in Tibetan areas (People's Republic of China 2009). The invasion mentioned in the definition is likewise evident in the 1950-51 Chinese invasion of Tibet, which resulted in the Seventeen Point Agreement[2] with the Dalai Lama, promising Tibetans the right to continue under their traditional governance in exchange for acceptance of Chinese sovereignty.[3] That this agreement was clearly an unequal agreement that the Dalai Lama could hardly refuse is another feature it shares with similar indigenous agreements around the world.

The UNDRIP identifies a number of standards that could appropriately be applied to assess prevailing conditions in Tibet. Its preliminary articles emphasize demilitarization of indigenous lands; the right of indigenous people to freely determine their relationship with states; that treaties, agreements, and constructive arrangements with states are matters of international concern; "the fundamental importance of the right of self-determination of all peoples, by virtue of which they freely determine their political status and freely pursue their economic, social and cultural development"; and that the right to exercise self-determination in conformity with international law shall not be denied. That Tibet is heavily militarized, and that the Tibetan people have never been allowed to make a free choice in determining their association with PRC, is widely appreciated. Efforts by the exiled Tibetan leadership to negotiate agreement concerning these issues have been consistently rebuffed. International concern over these matters has been the subject of numerous non-governmental organization, national, and international reports.

The UN Declaration, in its main text, guarantees indigenous peoples the right of self-determination; the right to autonomy or self-government in matters relating to their internal and local affairs; the right to manifest, practice, develop, and teach their spiritual and religious traditions, customs, and ceremonies, including private access to their religious and cultural sites and control of their ceremonial objects; the right to participate in decision-making in matters which would affect their rights, through representatives chosen by themselves in accordance with their own procedures; the right to be consulted and given prior consent through their own representative institutions before implementing state legislative and administrative measures; and the right to recognition, observance, and enforcement of treaties, agreements, and other constructive arrangements.[4] At the same time, they are guaranteed the rights protected by various human rights treaties and covenants. China's nationwide imposition of top-down authoritarian rule, its dismissive responses to Tibetan efforts at negotiation, and its weak general protection of basic human rights clearly fail to meet these standards. A closer look in the following section shows just how far China has strayed from these standards and even its own earlier commitments reflected in the Seventeen Point Agreement.

Tibetan "Autonomy" Under PRC Rule

The Seventeen Point Agreement that China imposed on Tibet when it occupied the country in 1950-51 actually came closer than any subsequent policies to the standards of the UNDRIP. The agreement acknowledged Tibet's special status, promised autonomy, and upheld Tibet's traditional system of self-rule. Chinese officials in the revolutionary zeal of the 1950s, however, showed little regard for these commitments, as they sought to impose "democratic reform" under Chinese Communist Party (CCP) rule, which they imagined Tibetans would quickly embrace. Chaffing under such an invasive approach, popular rebellion ensued and the Dalai Lama fled to India in March of 1959. There he established a government in exile that persists to the present (Dalai Lama 1991). If the Dalai Lama had stayed in Tibet, it seems likely that the Tibetan people and the world at large would have ultimately been deprived of one of the world's leading spiritual leaders.[5]

After the Dalai Lama fled into exile, PRC leaders abandoned their commitments under the Seventeen Point Agreement and established the Tibetan Autonomous Region (TAR) where, under the current Law on National Regional Autonomy (LRNA), central control clearly outweighs any notion of autonomy (China 1984 [2001]). About half of the contiguous traditional Tibetan areas have been distributed across 12 lesser autonomous areas in adjoining provinces, in what looks to Tibetans like a divide-and-conquer strategy. The large military presence, especially in the TAR, suggests the PRC views Tibet more in terms of national security than indigenous rights. The LRNA applies to all 55 designated national minorities, but the heavy-handed direct control practiced under its provisions seems targeted mostly at Tibet and the Uyghur areas in neighboring Xinjiang. A suspicious mind may wonder whether the generous designation of so many national minorities aims to water down such quasi-indigenous status.

The 1982 PRC Constitution, passed after the Cultural Revolution during China's liberalizing phase, appears to offer local autonomy. Article 4 provides that "Regional autonomy is practiced in areas where people of minority nationalities live in concentrated communities" (China 1982). As is replicated in the LRNA, such autonomy includes the power to enact "regulations on the exercise of autonomy (*zizhi tiaoli*) and other separate regulations (*danxing tiaoli*) in light of the political, economic and cultural characteristics." (China 1982; 1984).[6] "Regulations on the exercise of autonomy" are effectively a sub-constitution or basic law, and one such law would be enacted in each region. A difficulty has been the requirement of higher approval for all such laws enacted in autonomous regions. Such approval must typically come from the next higher level of government: for autonomous regions, the central government, and for autonomous prefectures and counties, the provincial government. None of the PRC's five autonomous regions – being Tibet, Xinjiang, Inner Mongolia, Guangxi, and Ningxia – have received approval for such basic regulation on the exercise of autonomy. The attempt to enact a basic regulation in the TAR went through 15 drafts and was eventually abandoned without being submitted to the State Council (Ghai and Woodman 2009). Autonomous prefectures and counties have received approval from provincial governments for basic autonomy laws, but these simply track the LRNA content, showing little evidence of local autonomy. Autonomous regions and other areas have enacted many "separate regulations."[7] A third category would be ordinary laws unrelated to autonomy, which do not require such higher approval.

The picture that emerges is one of strict central control. Beyond the official approval required for enactment of autonomous laws, this control is most substantially exercised through CCP oversight at all levels. CCP committees are required to approve draft legislation at every step in the legislative process (Xia 2009). Other factors that facilitate this careful control of political choice in such minority autonomous regions include the replication of national political structures, such as people's congresses and CCP oversight at all levels of autonomous government; the reality that Chinese cadres always hold the top CCP position in the regions; and, finally, a communist ideology that claims Chinese "liberation" of the area and effectively denies the indigenous reality of such regions.

The outcome has been decades of Chinese domination and repression in Tibetan regions. During periods of national political chaos and repression, such as the Cultural Revolution, the level of destruction has been palpable, breeding high levels of Tibetan resentment. While recent years have seen Chinese policy encourage economic development, these moves have not been met with the hoped-for Tibetan gratitude. Tibetans have tended to see these policies as self-serving efforts to facilitate resource extraction, open up

Chinese migration into Tibetan areas, and repress opposition – all favoring Chinese interests. Repressive efforts that have included close monitoring and "reeducation" in Tibetan monasteries, and a strong presence of security forces have bred even more resentment. Tibetan opposition has been manifest in various protests and even riots, and, most recently, in over 120 self-immolations (Davis 2012). Any pretext of carrying out the original promise of the Seventeen Point Agreement, or even current national minority laws, has largely evaporated. Current policies fall far short of the promise of the UNDRIP.

The Tibetan Memorandum and the Failure of Negotiation

The demonstrations and riots in 2008 came at a particularly inopportune time for the PRC, as it prepared to host the 2008 Olympics. Efforts at damage control led to three critical meetings straddling the Beijing Olympics in May, July, and October of 2008. For years the Dalai Lama had advocated what he labeled a "middle way" approach to achieving genuine autonomy for Tibet, an approach he urged could fit under the PRC Constitution (Central Tibetan Administration 2006). With the Beijing Olympics approaching, in the July 2008 meeting, Chinese officials asked the Dalai Lama's representatives to submit a memorandum indicating how their middle way approach would fit under the PRC Constitution. The Tibetan Memorandum on Genuine Autonomy for the Tibetan People was submitted to Chinese officials at the October 2008 meeting, which followed closely on the heels of the Beijing Olympics (Central Tibetan Administration 2008).[8]

The Tibetan memorandum outlined areas of hoped-for autonomy in eleven policy areas that largely tracked the autonomy areas identified in the PRC Constitution: language, culture, religion, education, environmental protection, utilization of natural resources, economic development and trade, public health, internal public security, population migration, and cultural, educational, and religious exchanges with other countries. In seeking local control over immigration and external relations in the commercial and cultural areas, the memorandum appeared to track the somewhat more robust autonomy afforded to Hong Kong and Macau under Article 31 of the PRC Constitution (China 1982). The memorandum also sought to avoid the central government approval process required under existing national minority laws. Finally, the memorandum sought to unify all contiguous Tibetan autonomous areas into one. All of these areas easily track the guidelines in the UNDRIP.

The official Chinese response to Tibetan overtures and the Memorandum clearly signaled the PRC's dismissal of the UNDRIP requirement of negotiating with freely chosen representatives of indigenous peoples. PRC officials promptly downgraded the discussions, indicating Sino-Tibetan "contacts and dialogues were about the Dalai Lama's personal future, and not so-called 'China-Tibet negotiation' or 'dialogue between Han and Tibetan people'" (*Xinhua*, 6 July 2008). The PRC's official aim was clearly damage control, as it insisted on three "stops" to "stop activities aimed at splitting China, stop plotting and inciting violence and stop disrupting and sabotaging the Beijing Olympic Games" (*Xinhua*, 6 July 2008). This was later refined to "four non-supports": "not to support activities to disturb the upcoming Beijing Olympic Games, not to support plots to fan violent criminal activities, not to support and concretely curb the violent terrorist activities of the 'Tibetan Youth Congress' and not to support any argument and activity to seek 'Tibet independence' and split the region from the country" (*Xinhua*, 6 July 2008). Chinese officials dismissively challenged the Dalai Lama's credentials to represent the Tibetan people, insisting that he must speak to the central government as a "common person" (*Indo-Asian News Service* 15 July 2008). They launched vociferous personal attacks, labeling the Dalai Lama a "wolf in monk's robes" (Davis 2008).

Responding directly to the Tibetan Memorandum, a State Council Address likened the Tibetan notion of "genuine autonomy" to the "high degree of autonomy" allowed Hong Kong.[9] The Tibetans were accused of seeking "half-independence" and "covert independence," though no explanation is given why the same language applied to Hong Kong means only autonomy. The State Council Address further accuses the exiled Tibetans of "colluding with such dregs as 'democracy activists', 'falunkun (Falungong) elements' and 'Eastern Turkistan terrorists.'" The Tibetan Memorandum's proposal to gain control over immigration into Tibet is likened to "ethnic cleansing." The State Council Address declared, "We never discussed the so-called 'Tibet issue' and will 'never make a concession.'" This language suggests the most extreme rejection of basic indigenous rights and associated autonomy for Tibetans.

Conclusion

Chinese officials responsible for Tibet policy, primarily in the PRC United Front Works Department, appear to see Tibet primarily as a security problem. Their views seem similar to historical colonialist policies, including a sense that they are bringing a superior culture and economic development to the region. One frequently hears Chinese expressions of concern about Tibetan ingratitude for generous Chinese investment in Tibetan areas. When this view is combined with Chinese claims of historical title to Tibet, Chinese outrage at the Tibetan challenge has left little room for compromise. The Dalai Lama, while offering compromise, has refused to bow to Chinese interpretations of Sino-Tibetan history. Chinese officials may conclude that such refusal will deprive any settlement of full legitimacy.

Confronted with the difficult reality of Chinese occupation, the Dalai Lama, as reflected in the Tibetan Memorandum, has offered to accept "genuine autonomy" under Chinese sovereignty. Chinese distrust of his representations, in the Memorandum and elsewhere, has left an impasse. The Dalai Lama has persisted in his efforts to reach compromise under his middle way approach, though skepticism about any breakthrough abounds. With his reservoir of support in the Tibetan community, Tibetans in exile have generally supported the Dalai Lama's efforts, though skepticism is growing within the Tibetan exile community. There is very little trust that the Chinese have any interest in compromise, the perception being that they are just biding their time, awaiting a post-Dalai Lama period when they expect the Tibetan exile movement to collapse.

The question to be asked is whether the Chinese are squandering the opportunity offered by the Dalai Lama, personally, and the Tibetan Memorandum, as a negotiating document, to reach a compromise. Should they take advantage of the Dalai Lama's ability to garner support in the Tibetan community for any agreement reached in line with international standards and the Tibetan Memorandum? Until their policies begin to measure up to international standards, such as reflected in the UNDRIP, their claims regarding Tibet and other critical minority areas will continue to meet global skepticism, even while their power has garnered formal recognition of their sovereignty over Tibet. Given the visibility of this issue in nearly every Chinese foreign policy outing, the price paid for these poorly conceived policies surely stretches beyond Tibet to skepticism in general about China's rise. Until the PRC acknowledges its international obligations, the deplorable human rights situation in Tibet seems destined to continue, as will a festering political sore covering nearly one-quarter of contemporary Chinese territory.

References

Central Tibetan Administration. (2006) *The Middle-Way Approach: A Framework for Resolving the Issue of Tibet*. Dharamsala, India: Department of Information and International Relations.

Central Tibetan Administration. (2008) *Memorandum on Genuine Autonomy for the Tibetan people*. Available at: http://tibet.net/important-issues/sino-tibetan-dialogue/memorandum-on-geniune-autonomy-for-the-tibetan-people/ (Accessed 7 January 2014).

Central Tibetan Administration. (2010) *Note on the Memorandum on Genuine Autonomy for the Tibetan People*. Available at: http://tibet.net/important-issues/sino-tibetan-dialogue/note-on-the-memorandum-on-genuine-autonomy-for-the-tibetan-people/ (Accessed 7 January 2014).

China. Fifth National People's Congress. (1982) *Constitution of the People's Republic of China*. Available at: http://english.peopledaily.com.cn/constitution/constitution.html (Accessed 7 January 2014).

China. Sixth National People's Congress (1984 [revised in 2001]) *Law of the People's Republic of China on Regional National Autonomy*. Available at: http://www.china.org. cn/english/government/207138.htm (Accessed 7 January 2014).

Crossley, P. (1999) *A Translucent Mirror: History and Identity in Qing Imperial Ideology*. Berkeley, California: University of California Press.

Dalai Lama. (1991) *Freedom in Exile: The Autobiography of the Dalai Lama*. New York: HarperCollins Publishers.

Davis, M.C. (2008) "For Talks to Succeed, China Must Admit to a Tibet Problem." *YaleGlobal Online*, May 16. Available at: http://yaleglobal.yale.edu/content/talks-succeed-china-must-admit-tibet-problem (Accessed 7 January 2014).

Davis, M.C. (2012) "Tibet and China's 'National Minority' Policies." *Orbis*, Summer 2012: 429–46.

Ghai, Y. and Woodman, S. (2009) "Unused Power: Contestation Over Autonomy Legislation in the PRC." *Pacific Affairs*, 82(1): 29–46.

People's Republic of China. Information Office of the State Council. (2009) *Fifty Years of Democratic Reform in Tibet*. White Paper. Available at: http://www.chinadaily.com.cn/china/2009-03/02/content_7527376.htm (Accessed 7 January 2014).

Smith, W.W., Jr. (1996) *Tibetan Nation: A History of Tibetan Nationalism and Sino-Tibetan Relations*. Boulder, Colorado: Westview.

Sperling, E. (2004) *The Tibetan-China Conflict: History and Polemics*. Washington, DC: East-West Center Washington.

UN Economic and Social Council. Sub-Commission on the Prevention of Discrimination and Protection of Minorities. (1986) *Study of the Problem of Discrimination Against Indigenous Peoples by Special Rapporteur José Martinez Cobo*. UN Doc. E/CN.4/Sub.2/1986/21/Add.8.

UN General Assembly. (2008) *United Nations Declaration on the Rights of Indigenous Peoples resolution / adopted by the General Assembly*. 2 October 2007, UN. Doc. A/RES/61/295.

Xia, C. (2009) "Autonomous Legislative Power in Regional Ethnic Autonomy of the People's Republic of China." In: Oliveira, J. and Cardinal P. eds. *One Country, Two Systems, Three Legal Orders: Perspectives of Evolution*. Berlin and Heidelberg: Springer-Verlag.

Endnotes

1. At the time of the Declaration there was thought to be over 370 million indigenous people worldwide (*International Herald Tribune* 13 September 2007).

2. The full title is the "Agreement of the Central People's Government and the Local Government of Tibet on Measures for the Peaceful Liberation of Tibet," which was signed on 23 May 1951.

3. The title of the agreement appears to suggest that China was just reclaiming an historical possession, but Tibetan resistance and numerous scholarly historical assessments call this into question (see Smith, Jr. 1996; Crossley 1999; Sperling 2004). In the present worldview, one might expect the efforts of one nationality to claim ownership over another nationality with its own distinctive culture and identity to be viewed with skepticism (see Davis 2012).

4. See UNDRIP Articles 3, 4, 12, 18, and 19 (UN General Assembly 2008).

5. The 10th Panchen Lama, the second highest Tibetan spiritual leader, who stayed behind to support Chinese rule wound up spending nearly two decades in prison or under house arrest and eventually died at age 51. His successor designated by the Dalai Lama disappeared as a child and has not reappeared since.

6. Such provision is repeated in Article 66 of the Legislative Law of China.

7. Separate regulations are made by autonomous legislative bodies on specific topics, such as language, marriage, family planning, and so on.

8. After Beijing responded to the Memorandum, the exiled government published a separate response note (see Central Tibetan Administration 2010).

9. Address at the Press Conference by the State Council Office, Beijing, 10 November 2008 (address given by Mr. Zhu Weiqun, Executive Vice-Minister of the United Front Work Department of the CPC Central Committee). The United Front Work Department is responsible for national minority affairs.

11

Tibetan Self-Determination: A Stark Choice for an Abandoned People

ROB DICKINSON
NEWCASTLE UNIVERSITY, UNITED KINGDOM

Tibet and the People's Republic of China

Self-determination of peoples – the right of peoples to determine their own political destiny (Kaczorowska 2010: 574) – reverberates around the world in the context both of peoples and nations trying to break away from the state in which they find themselves entrapped, and of peoples within states seeking greater rights for themselves against authoritarian rulers. Events in the Arab Spring have brought to the fore rebellion and also potential fragmentation of states. Yet all of this is nothing new.

As an example, the plight of the Tibetan people has attracted international attention for more than sixty years. The government of the People's Republic of China (PRC) sent troops into Tibet in 1950, completing a successful invasion – or liberation, depending on the viewpoint taken – in the autumn of 1951 when the People's Liberation Army entered Lhasa, the Tibetan capital. Tibetan proponents contend that this represented an invasion that ended the independence of Tibet (e.g. Goldstein 1989: 813); the PRC contends that "both the Chinese and Tibetan peoples were anxiously awaiting the region's 'liberation' from oppressive colonialism and reactionary exploitation" (Ginsburgs 1960: 339). Despite the attention Tibet has attracted, the Tibetan people find that they remain today within and a part of the PRC, the majority of historical Tibet forming the Tibet Autonomous Region. Self-determination does not always prove to be easy.

It may be asked why Tibet has failed to achieve the genuine autonomy it seeks, let alone separation from the PRC, and, indeed, the statehood it craves (Dickinson 2012). Kosovo might be seen as an example of an autonomous region that has in recent years achieved independence, and it has proved possible to overthrow governments in states such as Egypt (Dickinson 2012; 2013).

Ineffective Tibetan Claims

The ineffectiveness of Tibetan claims trace back to the 1950s: in 1950, no state came to the aid of the Tibetans and Tibet's claim for full political independence found no state support. No resolutions were passed by the United Nations (UN) Security Council or General Assembly at a time when states were preoccupied with the Korean question, the Korean War having broken out in June 1950. No UN General Assembly resolution succeeded until 1959, and only three in all have to date been passed.[1] These resolutions refer to the "fundamental human rights and freedoms" of the people of Tibet, and the second of the resolutions refers to "their right to self-determination." However, the PRC has not complied with the resolutions, and its current position as a Permanent Member of the UN Security Council appears to give it immunity in this context, reinforcing its claim that Tibet is an internal Chinese matter not brooking external interference. Member states of the UN have not been prepared to oppose the PRC over the issue of Tibet, and realism in the form of political self-interest has prevailed.

As Tibetan claims have languished, the PRC has gained in power over the last six decades, strengthening its hold on its territory. It has been criticised on numerous occasions for human rights abuses within its territory, for example with regard to Tibet and also with reference to the crackdown on protests in Tiananmen Square in 1989. Despite that, however, the prestige and position of the PRC has progressively been enhanced. The PRC is currently an elected member state of the UN Human Rights Council, and in the elections the candidate states' contribution "to the promotion and protection of human rights" was taken into account (UN General Assembly 2006).

If Tibetan claims have proved to be ineffective, what is needed to successfully achieve self-determination in the face of opposition from a parent state?

Prerequisites for Self-Determination

There has been increasing fragmentation of states over recent years, in parallel to increased integration as globalisation continues apace. This is incipient in, for example, Canada and Australia, where indigenous peoples seek greater powers, and has become transparent in the once-unified Soviet Union and also the former Yugoslavia, now both largely broken up into their constituent parts. The Soviet Union, though, consented to its own break-up, and a right to self-determination for its constituent republics was enshrined in its constitution. Thus, self-determination in the form of consensual secession determined the outcome of the collapse of Soviet power.

This may be contrasted with the PRC, which maintains its hold on power and whose constitution emphasises the unity of the country (for example, see Article 52 of the Constitution of China 1982). However, other multinational states have disintegrated along national or ethnic lines. Self-determination is likely to be the harbinger of "discontent, disorder and rebellion" (words of Robert Lansing, Secretary of State to Woodrow Wilson, cited in Talbott 2000: 15); indeed it is discontent that leads to a quest for self-determination in the first instance. Nevertheless, rebellion may be seen as key – and violent rebellion, at that. This is highlighted in the context of the former Yugoslavia. Declarations of independence came from Slovenia and Croatia in June 1991, and ultimately the state broke up into constituent parts in a surge of violence and what came to be known as "ethnic cleansing." One of the entities breaking away was, as indicated above, Kosovo. There are two points of significance for Tibet here. The first point is that an autonomous region of a state has been able to separate from a parent state. Although Kosovo's statehood has yet to be recognised by the international community and it has not been accorded membership of the UN, more than half of UN Members have formally or informally recognised the Republic of Kosovo and the list is growing (Wolff and Rodt 2013). The second point is that violent rebellion may be seen as a prerequisite for unilateral secession from a parent state – and secession is the logical extreme of external self-determination (Dickinson 2014). That violent civil disobedience is a genuine and credible strategy for entities seeking self-determination is evidenced further by the only other entity that has, arguably, successfully achieved secession in opposition to its parent state: Bangladesh.

It is feasible, therefore, to say that non-consensual secession – external self-determination – is characterised by violent revolution. Internal self-determination, the right of a people to govern through autonomy, forms the second strand of self-determination. This, too, can be characterised by violence, as has been only too evident from 2011 onwards in the events of the Arab Spring, for example, in Egypt, Libya and Syria. Syria is particularly interesting in this regard as the state spirals into disorder and civil war. Militant groups achieve ascendancy, and fragmentation of the state appears ever more likely.

Thus, from each aspect of contested self-determination, external and internal, it can be argued that violent revolution is a precondition, a precursor, and, apparently, an essential ingredient. It is not, however, sufficient. Beyond this, there needs to be the support of the people; a case made for self-determination and accepted by the people. This is necessary with reference to either secession or internal self-determination, the latter potentially leading to the overthrow of the government. Even then, the case for self-determination, the support of the people for self-determination, and the violent revolution may prove insufficient, as instanced in the unfolding situation in Egypt.

Beyond these factors, support of the international community is significant. Such support has already been noted in the case of Kosovo, where the final outcome is as yet unresolved, although the momentum towards the ultimate recognition of Kosovo through membership of the UN seems clear. Of course, Bangladesh received international support, including initially military support from India, at the time of its violent secession from Pakistan,[2] and was admitted to membership of the UN on 17 September 1974. International support is also relevant where internal self-determination through overthrow of an existing regime is sought. For example, in the Arab Spring, the opposition found international support in overthrowing the authoritarian regime of Colonel Gaddafi in Libya; in Syria, little international support was forthcoming for the revolutionaries and, for the time being, President al-Assad remains in power.

The impact of the Internet and social media may also prove to be of significance, both in terms of rallying support to the cause and in garnering international support, for as the age of social media dawns, people become ever more aware of the plight of others. States are no longer the sole controllers of reaction to events, and the news agenda is not so much driven by the traditional mass media, but the ability of the masses to go on-line and inform the minds of others. Those who wish to inform can. This has become evident in the context of the Arab Spring, for instance, in Egypt, where Facebook campaigns were used to mobilise and underpin civil disobedience (Dickinson 2013: 64). Not all states, though, will be susceptible to media campaigns, whether campaigns of the traditional media or the new media.

Tibet

Some peoples, as demonstrated, have achieved secession in the face of parent state opposition, and some governments have been successfully overthrown. Tibet, however, is an entity that seems to have been left well behind in the self-determination stakes. A consideration of the prerequisites for self-determination demonstrates clearly why this has been the case.

First, it has been premised that violent rebellion, setting in force revolution, is a precursor of self-determination, and apparently an essential ingredient, although not sufficient in itself. There has been, in Tibet, sporadic violence and insurrection during the last sixty years and more. The 1950-51 invasion and liberation was not unopposed; further, insurrection broke out, for instance, in 1958 and 1959, and also in 1987 and 1988. Nevertheless, sustained, forceful, and effective rebellion against a powerful state, such as the PRC, intent on maintaining the integrity of its territory and the unity of the country, is impractical – and may be contrasted with the success achieved by Kosovo in breaking free from Serbia, the rump successor state of Yugoslavia. There is a qualitative difference between the size and power of the PRC, on the one hand, and Serbia – or, indeed, Yugoslavia in its earlier incarnation – on the other.

Moreover, Tibetans have not found support for their cause in the international arena. Just as at the outset, in the 1950s, the international situation on the Korean peninsula trumped the issue of Tibet and there was little support then for the Tibetan position, no international support would be found now for a violent revolution as the PRC takes its place in the mainstream of human rights protection and grows in confidence. In addition, governments of states such as the United States of America (USA) and Russia deem it is not in their best interests to oppose the PRC over Tibet: for example, the USA pursues its economic self-interest and Russia is mindful of the need to protect its own position in the face of actions by Chechen separatists. As a further point to note, and as a deterrent to international support for the Tibetans, the United Kingdom government felt the wrath of the PRC following a meeting of Prime Minister David Cameron with the Dalai Lama, Tibet's spiritual leader, in 2013 (Moore and Quinn 2013).

Neither the USA nor Russia – both major powers in the world – would wish to set the agenda and engage directly with the power of the PRC over an issue such as self-rule for the indigenous Tibetans. Indeed, in contrast to the majority of states that have, in one way or another, recognised the Republic of Kosovo, no state today recognises Tibet as an independent state.

To achieve secession or genuine autonomy against the wishes of a parent state, or to overthrow an existing regime outside the ballot box, it is argued that an entity needs first to have a clear and cohesive case to buttress its argument, to back that up with violent revolution, today successfully utilising social media to establish support for its claims, and attract international support to its cause. Tibetan society is founded on Buddhism and non-violence. That, in itself, ensures that widespread, cohesive Tibetan support for concerted violence is unlikely; violent revolution seems certain to fail in this instance in the face of the powerful PRC and, indeed, could premise the destruction of Tibet and the Tibetan people. This is a stark choice indeed. As a people, Tibetans have been abandoned to their fate by the international community.

References

China. Fifth National People's Congress. (1982) *Constitution of the People's Republic of China.* Available at: http://english.peopledaily.com.cn/constitution/constitution.html (Accessed 7 January 2014).

Crawford, J. (2006) *The Creation of States in International Law.* 2nd ed. Oxford: Clarendon Press.

Dickinson, R.A. (2012) "The Global Reach and Limitations of Self-Determination." *Cardozo Journal of International and Comparative Law,* 20(2): 367–98.

Dickinson, R.A. (2013) "Transformation of the Modern State: State Sovereignty and Human Rights in the Internet Age." *Connecticut Journal of International Law* 29(1): 51–68.

Dickinson, R.A. (2014) "Responsibility to Protect: Arab Spring Perspectives." *Buffalo Human Rights Law Review,* 20: 91-123.

Ginsburgs, G. (1960) "Peking – Lhasa – New Delhi." *Political Science Quarterly,* 75(3): 338–54.

Goldstein, M.C. (1989) *A History of Modern Tibet 1913-1951: The Demise of the Lamaist State.* Berkeley: University of California Press.

Kaczorowska, A. (2010) *Public International Law,* 4th ed. London: Routledge.

Moore, M. and Quinn, J. (2013) "David Cameron's rift with China could cost UK billions." *The Telegraph,* 6 May. Available from: http://www.telegraph.co.uk/news/politics/david-cameron/10040319/David-Camerons-rift-with-China-could-cost-UK-billions.html (Accessed 7 January 2014).

Talbott, S. (2000). "Self-Determination in an Interdependent World." *Foreign Policy,* 118: 152–63.

UN General Assembly. (2006) *Human Rights Council resolution / adopted by the General Assembly.* 3 April 2007, UN. Doc. A/RES/60/251.

Wolff, S. and Rodt, A.P. (2013) "Self-Determination After Kosovo." *Europe-Asia Studies,* 65(5): 799–822.

Endnotes

1. These are United Nations General Assembly Resolutions 1353 (XIV) in 1959, 1723 (XVI) in 1961, and 2079 (XX) in 1965.
2. Not all commentators are of the view that Bangladesh falls within the principle of self-determination, preferring the view that Bangladesh emerged "as a *fait accompli* achieved as a result of foreign military assistance in special circumstances" (Crawford 2006: 415-6).

12

Self-Determination: A Perspective from Abya Yala

EMILIO DEL VALLE ESCALANTE
COMUNIDAD DE ESTUDIOS MAYAS /
UNIVERSITY OF NORTH CAROLINA AT CHAPEL HILL, USA

For those unfamiliar with the term Abya Yala, the concept emerged toward the end of the 1970s in *Dulenega*, or what, for others, is today San Blas, Panama, a Kuna Tule territory.[1] Abya Yala in the Kuna language means "land in its full maturity." The Kuna believe that there are four cycles of life that have developed the planet earth: Kualagun Yala, Tagargun Yala, Tingua Yala, and Ahia or Abya Yala. Today, we are living in the last cycle of life. After the Kuna won a lawsuit to stop the construction of a shopping mall in Dulenega, they told a group of reporters that they employed the term Abya Yala to refer to the American continent in its totality. After listening to this story, Takir Mamani, the Bolivian Aymara leader, and Tupaj Katari, one of the founders of the indigenous rights movement in Bolivia, suggested that indigenous peoples and indigenous organizations use the term Abya Yala in their official declarations to refer to the American continent. He argues that recognizing and "placing foreign names on our villages, our cities, and our continents is equivalent to subjecting our identities to the will of our invaders and their heirs" (Arias et al. 2012: 7, my translation). Therefore, renaming the continent would be the first step toward epistemic decolonization and the establishment of indigenous peoples' autonomy and self-determination. Since the 1980s, many indigenous activists, writers, and organizations have embraced Mamani's suggestion, and Abya Yala has become a way not only to refer to the continent, but also a differentiated indigenous locus of cultural and political expression (Muyolema 2001: 329).

The struggles of the Kuna epitomize the struggles of Indigenous rights movements on the continent to defend and maintain their territories and freely determine their own economic, social, and cultural development. Indeed, these movements have invoked "the concept of self-determination in formulating demands against actual or perceived oppression of the status quo," and the necessity of establishing themselves as distinct sovereign peoples, with historical rights to their lands (Anaya 1993: 131). These struggles to dignify Indigenous identities and territories have been fought historically on many fronts. They include armed struggles, non-violent activism, accepting government jobs to gain degrees of self-government, or electoral politics in pursuit of making change from above. In this article, I explore the question of self-determination in Abya Yala by focusing on the Zapatista Army of National Liberation (EZLN) in Chiapas, Mexico, and the Movement Toward Socialism (MAS) in Bolivia. These two movements are perhaps the most referenced within discussions of indigenous self-determination, sovereignty, and autonomy in the south of Abya Yala. In their approaches to indigenous rights to land and resources, both the EZLN and MAS allow us to critically explore what is at stake in our efforts to overcome (neo)colonialism.

The Zapatistas and the Politics of *mandar obedeciendo*

The EZLN is a Maya social movement that emerged in January 1994 as a response to the signing of the North American Free Trade Agreement (NAFTA) between the governments of Mexico, the United States, and Canada. During the initial revolt, the Zapatistas wore ski masks to protect the identity of its members against institutional repression, and to express a non-hierarchical, more egalitarian political and organizational structure. Today, the ski mask symbolizes their historical marginalization and their struggle to overcome it. Their name, Zapatistas, comes from the Nahuatl peasant leader Emiliano Zapata (1879-1911), one of the leading figures of the Mexican Revolution of 1910 that overthrew the dictatorship of Porfirio Díaz.[2] The EZLN began as an armed movement declaring war against the Mexican nation-state, but later turned into a social movement that struggles to promote basic human rights and a level of political and cultural autonomy within Mexico. Since developing into a social movement, they have established that they do not want to become a democratic political party, since this would perpetuate a political system that, by gaining power, distances itself from the needs of the people, especially those at the margins. They have, therefore, maintained independence from political parties and the state, promoting instead a mandate of *mandar obedeciendo* (command by obeying), attempting to transform the political system into one that raises the consciousness of civil society to address the needs and demands of the historically marginalized within modern societies. They have developed a discourse that addresses the major critical problems that affect not only indigenous peoples, but all those who suffer repression, poverty, discrimination, and political and economic marginalization. This is exemplified by Subcomandante Marcos, one of the spokespersons of the movement, when he explains the symbolism of his own political subjectivity as a masked dissident:

> Marcos is gay in San Francisco, black in South Africa, Asian in Europe, Chicano in San Isidro, anarchist in Spain, Palestinian in Israel, Indigenous in the streets of San Cristóbal... Jew in Germany... feminist in political parties, Communist in the post-Cold War era, prisoner in Cintalapa, pacifist in Bosnia, Mapuche in the Andes... unemployed worker... rebellious student, dissident in neoliberalism... Marcos is all the minorities who are untolerated, oppressed, resisting, exploding, saying "Enough." [A]ll that makes power and good consciences uncomfortable, that is Marcos (Marcos 1995: 214–5).

By making effective use of the mass media, the Zapatistas have been able to attract global attention and achieve a level of global solidarity that has fuelled their uprising for over twenty years. They are the only movement in Mexico that has been able to successfully connect and universalize their struggle for justice in and outside the country.

While initially the EZLN tried to promote its demands through negotiations with the Mexican government, peace talks came to an end in April 2001. Their demands, which included the implementation of Indigenous Accords, such as land tenure, health, and indigenous education, were not addressed by then president, Vicente Fox (2000-2006). They went into "silence," and in 2003 declared the birth of *Caracoles* (snails), which marked the beginning of Zapatista autonomous communities within the territories they control. They broke relations with all political parties, including the "leftist progressive" Party of the Democratic Revolution (PRD) and their representative, Manuel López Obrador, who, some argue, lost the elections in 2006 due to losing Zapatista support.[3]

In December 2012, the EZLN mobilized thousands of Indigenous Zapatistas, peacefully taking five municipalities in Chiapas. They published an official communiqué at the end of the month, announcing how, after decades of struggle, they successfully created self-sufficient and autonomous communities with their own political projects and objectives, independent of the Mexican nation-state. They indicate, "We don't need them [Political parties and the nation-state] in order to survive" (Marcos 2012). Since becoming autonomous communities, they boast that they have significantly strengthened and improved their material conditions. They underscore, among other achievements, that their standards of living are "higher than those of the indigenous communities that support the governments in office, who receive handouts that are squandered on alcohol and useless items." Zapatista homes, they state, "have improved without damaging nature... Our sons and daughters go to a school that teaches them their own history, that of their country and that of the world, as well as the sciences and techniques necessary for them to grow without ceasing to be indigenous" (Marcos 2012).

On 1 January 2014, the Zapatistas celebrated the twentieth anniversary of their initial uprising. Their revolution and struggle for self-determination has combined armed struggle and the effective use of the media to spread an ideological discourse that has been attractive to many, precisely because it proposes distance from electoral politics. They identify the nation-state and its established structures as naturally imbricated in economic, political, and cultural systems that reify hierarchical structures based on the domination of certain ethnic/racial and social groups. Self-determination, in this sense, is "understood as a means of gaining distance or protection from rather than inclusion in state institutions... [They] express a profound sense of alienation toward these institutions, which carry the stigma of colonial domination" (Murphy 2008: 186). The Zapatistas even posit themselves as a global example of resistance and self-determination, indicating that their struggle represents "a new form of social life" that "attracts the attention of honest people all over the planet" (Marcos 2012). They insist that they will maintain a "critical distance with respect to the entirety of the Mexican political class which has thrived at the expense of the needs and desires of humble and simple people" (Marcos 2012).

MAS: Self-Determination and the Path of Electoral Politics

The Movement Toward Socialism (MAS) in Bolivia grew out of the *Cocaleros* (Coca leaf growers) popular movement in the region of El Chapare. It is a movement highly influenced by the *Confederación Sindical Única de Trabajadores Campesinos de Bolivia* (Unitary Syndical Confederation of Peasant Workers of Bolivia – CSUTCB), and their struggle for improved agricultural policies.[4] In 1989, the Cocaleros allied with *Izquierda Unida*, or United Left (IU), in order to gain political prominence in local municipalities. In 1995, they created the assembly "Political tool for the Sovereignty of the Common People" (IPSP), which later turned into the electoral political party MAS (Dangl 2007: 49). The movement gained national prominence in 1997 with its resistance to President Hugo Banzer's neoliberal privatization policies, particularly Law 1008, which declared a "zero coca" policy in Bolivia (Crabtree 2005:38). Out of the struggle to defend the growing and production of the coca leaf, the Aymara coca farmer Evo Morales rose in political standing and became the MAS leader. Given public discontent with neoliberal policies and politics, MAS political discourses – based on "anti-neoliberalism," "anti-imperialism," and multiculturalism – were well received by large sectors of the Bolivian population who voted them into national office with 53.74% of the popular vote.

In his inauguration speech as Bolivian President on 21 January 2006, Morales evoked the words of the Zapatistas by indicating that his government would be based on the "Command by obeying" mandate. He told thousands of Bolivians that his presidency would be the first step to ending the "colonial state and the neoliberal model," and made reference to the rights of Indigenous Peoples in Bolivia (Aymaras, Quechuas, Guaranies, Mojeños, Chapacos, Vallunos, Chiquitanos, Yuracarés, Chipayas, and Muratos) as the true and absolute owners of the land. Invoking the right to self-determination and the sovereignty of Bolivia as a free nation-state, Morales proposed the nationalization of resources like natural gas, oil, and minerals. "We have the obligation to industrialize our national resources in order to get out of poverty," he said (Morales 2006, my translation). In a 2008 interview, he indicated how, after natural reserves were nationalized, the country began to receive $8 billion annually, in contrast to the $1 billion they received prior to 2005 (Goodman et al. 2008). The wealth in the hands of the state, from Morales' perspective, now served to create social programs to benefit the population. Despite criticism regarding the nationalization of resources, Morales' presidency and his policies gained much support. In 2009, he was re-elected president for a second term in office, winning with over 60% of the national vote.

Morales' biggest challenge on the other hand came in 2011, when his government proposed the construction of a highway that would run through the *Parque Nacional y Territorio Indígena y Parque Nacional Isiboro Sécure*, or Isiboro Sécure National Park and Indigenous Territory (TIPNIS). This territory, which encompasses 1.2 million hectares of land, is inhabited by Amazonian Indigenous nations like the Mojeños-Trinitarios, Chimanes, and Yuracarés in the North, and by Quechua and Aymaras in the South. The latter are called *colonizadores* (colonizers) since they migrated to and established themselves in the region in the 1970s (Webber 2012). Morales' decision to build the highway led to a 65-day march in August 2011 by Amazonian indigenous nations to La Paz to protest the project. Initially, the marches were denounced by the government as an "imperialist conspiracy," and were violently repressed in September 2011 (Webber 2012). Morales insisted "that the road was needed to bring economic development to poor [Amazonian] indigenous communities" (Frantz 2011). However, as the protests grew to the point of acquiring national and international attention, Morales gave in to the demands and, in December of the same year, signed the *intangible* (untouchable) law, which states that the national park cannot be exploited by commercial enterprises. The decision, however, led to new protests by indigenous sectors that had supported Morales' initial decision and represented his constituency, like The *Consejo Indígena del Sur* (Indigenous Council of the South – CONISUR), residents of Cochabamba and San Ignacio de Moxos, and Cocaleros (Frantz 2011). The conflict showed the tensions between the various indigenous peoples and, at the same time, some of the contradictions of Morales' socialist and sovereign agenda.

Indeed, while Morales proposes to "change the colonial state" because it is based on "plundering, exploiting and marginalizing" important sectors of the Bolivian population, the TIPNIS affair displays how his economic agenda still depends on extractivism; that is, the exploitation and exportation of natural resources that are used in capitalist international markets (Gudynas 2009: 190). While these policies have indeed created profound political changes that have benefited sectors of the population with the improvement and implementation of social programs, with his ideas of "poverty" and "progress," Morales still endorses a Eurocentric discourse that sees Mother Earth as an entity that can be "exploited" to end poverty. In this sense, his economic policies characterize themselves as some form of more humane capitalism. The problem, however, is that they are still capitalist and have maintained divisions among Indigenous sectors. These types of policies have led some scholars, like Silvia Rivera Cusicanqui, to argue that Morales' presidency represents the interests of an elitist and commercial capitalist class (Dulce 2014). She goes as far as to indicate that Morales is not an indigenous leader, and that there are no indigenous presidents in Latin America.

Conclusion

In January 2006, after Morales was elected President of Bolivia, he invited the EZLN's leadership to his presidential inauguration. The Zapatistas declined the invitation. In an interview months later, Subcomandante Marcos explained that the EZLN does not look toward "the Bolivia of above, but, rather, the Bolivia from below. And these are the values that are taken into account: those of the popular movement that caused Bolivia to crash and opened the possibility that the government of Evo could decide for one side or the other" (Rodríguez Lascano 2006). The statement defines the two distinct paths followed by MAS and the EZLN in their efforts to establish self-determination and autonomy for indigenous peoples. Both movements, in their own ways, represent struggles that occur "within the structure of domination *vis a vis* techniques of government, by exercising their freedom of thought and action with the aim of modifying the system in the short term and transforming it from within in the long term" (Tully 2000: 50).

Despite their differences, both movements display the challenges of transcending (neo)colonialism. As Cherokee theologian William Baldridge states, for indigenous peoples "the most pervasive result of colonialism is that we cannot even begin a conversation without referencing our words to definitions imposed or rooted in 1492" (Weaver 2001: 292). These movements show that, whatever political road is taken, the path toward self-determination necessarily involves negotiating with the nation-state and its hegemonic institutions. While attempts to break free have involved enormous sacrifices characterized by the loss of lives, as well as psychological and epistemological violence, the EZLN and MAS represent options in a "globalized" world that continues to threaten our existence. Yet, the debates and discussions and respective struggles give us the hope and dignity necessary to one day recover our territories, and use them according our own needs so our cultures and peoples continue flourishing. They also allow us to think of the possibility of materializing our own civilizational project: Abya Yala.

References

Anaya, J. (1993) "A Contemporary Definition of the International Norm of Self-Determination." *Transnational Law and Contemporary Problems,* 131(3): 31–164.

Arias, A., Cárcamo-Huechante, L.E., and del Valle Escalante, E. (2012) "Literaturas de Abya Yala." *LASA Forum,* 43(1): 7–10.

Collier, G. A. (2005) *Basta! Land and the Zapatista Rebellion in Chiapas.* 3rd ed. Oakland, California: Food First Books.

Crabtree, J. (2005) *Patterns of Protest: Politics and Social Movements in Bolivia.* London: Latin American Bureau.

Dangl, B. (2007) *The Price of Fire: Resource Wars and Social Movements in Bolivia.* Edinburgh, United Kingdom: AK Press.

Dulce, D. d. a. (2014). *Silvia Rivera Cusicanqui: "Evo está en el corazón de la derecha". Territorios en resistencia.* Available at: http://www.territoriosenresistencia.org/ noticias/silvia-rivera-cusicanqui-evo-esta-en-el-corazon-de-la-derecha (Accessed 15 January 2014).

Dunkerley, J. (2007) "Evo Morales, the 'Two Bolivias' and the Third Bolivian Revolution." *Journal of Latin American Studies,* 39: 133–66.

Frantz, C. (2011) *Council on Hemispheric Affairs. The TIPNIS Affair: Indigenous Conflicts and the Limits on "Pink Tide" States Under Capitalist Realities.* Available at: http://www.coha.org/the-tipnis-affair-indigenous-conflicts-and-the-limits-on-pink-tide-states-under-capitalist-realities/ (Accessed 15 December 2013).

Goodman, A., Gonzalez, J., and Morales, E. (2008) "An Hour with Bolivian President Evo Morales: 'Neoliberalism Is No Solution for Humankind.'" *Democracy Now.* Available at: http://www.democracynow.org/2008/11/18/an_hour_with_bolivian_president_evo (Accessed 10 January 2014).

Gudynas, E. (2009) "Diez tesis urgentes sobre el nuevo extractivismo. Contextos y demandas bajo el progresismo sudamericano actual." In: Schuldt, J., Acosta, A., Barandiarán, Bebbington, A., Folchi, M., Alayza, A., and Gudynas, E. eds. *Extractivismo, política y sociedad.* Quito, Ecuador: CAAP and CLAES.

Harten, S. (2011) *The Rise of Evo Morales and the MAS.* London: Zed Books.

Hayden, T. E. (2002) *The Zapatista Reader.* New York: Nation Books.

Howe, J. (1998) *A People Who Would Not Kneel: Panama, the United States, and the San Blas Kuna.* Washington, District of Colombia: Smithsonian Institution Press.

Marcos, S. and León, J.P.D. (2001) *Our Word Is Our Weapon: Selected Writings.* New York: Seven Stories Press.

Marcos, S. (2004) *Ya basta! 10 Years of the Zapatista Uprising.* Edinburgh, United Kingdom: AK Press.

Marcos, S. (1995) *Shadows of Tender Fury: The Letters and Communiqués of Subcomandante Marcos and the Zapatista Army of National Liberation.* New York: Monthly Review Press.

Marcos, S. (2012) *Enlace Zapatista. EZLN ANNOUNCES THE FOLLOWING STEPS. Communiqué of December 30 2012.* Available at: http://enlacezapatista.ezln.org.mx/2013/01/02/ezln-announces-the-following-steps-communique-of-december-30-2012/ (Accessed 10 December 2013).

Morales, E. (2006) *Los discursos de Evo Morales.* Available at: http://www.aporrea.org/internacionales/n72540.html (Accessed 20 December 2013).

Murphy, M. (2008) "Representing Indigenous Self-Determination." *University of Toronto Law Journal,* 58(2): 185–216.

Muyolema, A. (2001) "De la 'cuestión indígena' a lo 'indígena' como cuestionamiento. Hacia una crítica del latinoamericanismo, el indigenismo y el mestiz(o)aje." In: Rodríguez, I. ed. *Convergencia de tiempos. Estudios subalternos/contextos latinoamericanos estado, cultura, subalternidad.* Amsterdam: Rodopi.

Rodríguez Lascano, S. (2006) *The Narco News Bulletin.* Available at: http://www.narconews.com/Issue41/article1861.html (Accessed 10 January 2014).

Salvador, M. L. (2002) *The Art of Being Kuna: Layers of Meaning Among the Kuna of Panama.* Seattle, WA: University of Washington Press.

Tully, J. (2000) "The Struggles of Indigenous Peoples for and of Freedom." In: Ivison, D., Patton, P., and Sanders, W. eds. *Political Theory and the Rights of Indigenous Peoples.* Cambridge: Cambridge University Press.

Weaver, J. (2001) *Other Words: American Indian Literature, Law, and Culture.* Norman, Oklahoma: University of Oklahoma Press.

Webber, J. R. (2011) *From Rebellion to Reform in Bolivia: Class Struggle, Indigenous Liberation, and the Politics of Evo Morales.* Chicago: Haymarket Books.

Webber, J. R. (2012) *International Socialism. Revolution against "progress": the TIPNIS struggle and class contradictions in Bolivia.* Available at: http://www.isj.org.uk/?id=780 (Accessed 15 December 2013).

Endnotes

1. "Dulenega" in the Kuna Tule language means the homeland of the people ("dule" means people and "nega" home, habitat, or homeland). For additional information about the Kuna peoples, see Howe (1998) and Salvador (2002).

2. The bibliography on the EZLN is extensive. For examples, see Collier (2005), Hayden (2002), and Marcos (1995; 2004). Most of the EZLN's manifestos and official communiqués can be found online at: http://www.ezln.org.mx/ and http://enlacezapatista.ezln.org.mx/. They also have created the monthly online journal, *Revista rebeldia*, which is available at: http://revistarebeldia.org/.

3. The break with López Obrador and the PRD occurred on 10 April 2004. The EZLN claims that PRD sympathizers and officials ambushed a group of Zapatistas that was commemorating Emiliano Zapata in the region of Zinacantan. They were also denied access to water. The incident was neither addressed nor resolved when it was raised with López Obrador.

4. The bibliography on MAS and Evo Morales is very extensive. For examples, see Crabtree (2005), Dangl (2007), Dunkerley (2007), and Harten (2011).

Contributors

Else Grete Broderstad is the Academic Director at the Centre for Sami Studies at the University of Tromsø – The Arctic University of Norway. She is part of the cross-disciplinary project TUNDRA, where she focuses on circumpolar governance arrangements, indigenous rights, and political participation. She is primarily interested in political procedures and rights governing the relationship between indigenous minorities and non-indigenous majorities. In her most recent publication, "Cross-border Reindeer Husbandry: Between Ancient Usage Rights and State Sovereignty," in *The Proposed Nordic Saami Convention. National and International Dimensions of Indigenous Property Rights*, edited by Nigel Bankes and Timo Koivurova (Hart Publishing, 2013), she discusses the problems of reaching an agreement between Norway and Sweden on cross-border reindeer husbandry management.

Michael Davis, a Professor in the Law Faculty at the University of Hong Kong, has held visiting chairs at Northwestern University Law School (2005-06) and Notre Dame Law School (2004-05), as well as the Schell Senior Fellowship at the Yale Law School (1994-95). His publications include *Constitutional Confrontation in Hong Kong* (Palgrave Macmillan, 1990), *Human Rights and Chinese Values* (Oxford University Press, 1995) and *International Intervention: From Power Politics to Global Responsibility* (ME Sharpe, 2004), as well as numerous articles in leading academic journals in law and political science. He has law degrees from the University of California, Hastings (JD) and Yale Law School (LLM).

Marisa Elena Duarte received her PhD in information science from the University of Washington. While there, she co-founded the Indigenous Information Research Group, a team of seven Native and Indigenous doctoral researchers examining problems of information, knowledge, and technology in Native and Indigenous communities. She is currently advancing a research agenda on the processes and social impacts of weaving the infrastructure for mobile information and communication technologies into Indian Country. She is a past co-chair of the Tribal Telecom & Technology Summit, and is a current postdoctoral fellow with the Program in American Indian & Indigenous Studies at the University of Illinois, Urbana-Champaign. She is also a member of the Pascua Yaqui Tribe.

Jeff Corntassel (Cherokee Nation) received his Ph.D. in Political Science from the University of Arizona in 1998, and is currently Associate Professor and Director of Indigenous Governance at the University of Victoria. His research and teaching interests include sustainable self-determination and Indigenous political mobilization. His research has been published in *Alternatives, Decolonization, Human Rights Quarterly, and Social Science Journal*. His first book, entitled *Forced Federalism: Contemporary Challenges to Indigenous Nationhood* (2008, University of Oklahoma Press), examines how Indigenous nations in the U.S. have mobilized politically as they encounter new threats to their governance from state policymakers. His next book is an edited volume in collaboration with Kanaka Maoli professors in Indigenous Politics at the University of Hawai'i, Manoa, and is entitled *Everyday Acts of Resurgence: People, Places, Practices*.

Ravi de Costa is an Associate Professor in the Faculty of Environmental Studies at York University, Toronto, Canada. His work centres on the institutional and cultural contexts of Indigenous-settler relations in Australia and Canada, with publications on treaty-making, reconciliation and apologies, and conflicts over land. He currently holds a Social Science and Humanities Research Council Standard (SSHRC) grant to examine the work of the Canadian Truth and Reconciliation Commission. He has also written extensively on the global movement of Indigenous peoples and the UN Declaration on the Rights of Indigenous Peoples.

Emilio del Valle Escalante (K'iche' Maya, Guatemala) is a member of Comunidad de Estudios Mayas and an Associate Professor of Spanish at the University of North Carolina, Chapel Hill. He is the author of *Maya Nationalisms and Postcolonial Challenges in Guatemala: Coloniality, Modernity and Identity Politics* (School for Advanced Research Press, 2009). He has also edited "Teorizando las literaturas indígenas" (a special issue of *A contracorriente*, 2013), and *U'k'ux kaj, u'k'ux ulew: Antologia de poesia Maya guatemalteca contemporanea* (2010).

Rob Dickinson is a Lecturer in Law at Newcastle Law School, Newcastle University, Newcastle upon Tyne, NE1 7RU, England, UK, email: rob.dickinson@ncl.ac.uk. Formerly a practising lawyer, he was appointed to the lectureship in 2008. His current research focuses on self-determination and human rights and on issues arising with reference to state sovereignty. His recently published work addresses issues arising out of the events of the Arab Spring, considering, *inter alia*, the impact of the Internet on state sovereignty, and also important issues of legitimacy of government and external interference in the affairs of a state in the context of the emerging doctrine of the Responsibility to Protect.

Hassan O. Kaya is Director of the Department of Science and Technology (DST) – National Research Foundation (NRF) Centre of Excellence in Indigenous Knowledge Systems (IKS) in South Africa. He is also a Patron of the African Young Scientists Initiative on Climate Change and Indigenous Knowledge Systems. He holds a PhD in Sociology of Development (Freie Universität, Berlin, Germany) and Bachelors (Honours) and Masters Degrees in Development Studies (University of Dar es Salaam, Tanzania). He has researched, presented papers, lectured, and initiated various IKS-related community projects. He has recently published "African Indigenous Knowledge Systems and Relevance of Higher Education in South Africa" (*International Education Journal,* 2013).

Michael Murphy is an Associate Professor in the Political Science Department at the University of Northern British Columbia, where he holds the Canada Research Chair in Comparative Indigenous-State Relations. His research is currently focused on questions of state-indigenous reconciliation, and the relationship between self-determination and the health and well-being of indigenous communities around the globe. His most recent publications include "Apology, Recognition and Reconciliation" (*Human Rights Review,* 2011), *Multiculturalism. A Critical Introduction* (Routledge, 2012), and "Self-Determination as a Collective Capability: The Case of Indigenous Peoples" (*Journal of Human Development and Capabilities,* 2014).

Dominic O'Sullivan is an Associate Professor in political science at Charles Sturt University, Australia. His research is primarily in comparative indigenous politics and policy, and his extensive publications include three books: *Faith, Politics and Reconciliation: Catholicism and the politics of indigeneity* (ATF Press, 2005), *Beyond Biculturalism: the politics of an indigenous minority* (Huia Publishers, 2007) and, with Russell Bishop and Mere Berryman, *Scaling up education reform: addressing the politics of disparity* (NZCER Press, 2010). Dominic is from the Te Rarawa and Ngati Kahu iwi of northern New Zealand.

Manuela Lavinas Picq is Professor of International Relations at the Universidad San Francisco de Quito, Ecuador. Her research focuses on the role of gender and Indigeneity in the practice and study of world politics. She is currently a Member at the Institute for Advanced Study, where she is finishing a book locating Indigenous women politics in international relations and starting a project about the Amazon as a cosmopolitan space.

Roderic Pitty is an Associate Professor of International Relations at the University of Western Australia, teaching in global governance and European international politics. He has written reports on Aboriginal deaths in custody in Australia and has reviewed the conditions required for establishing a treaty relationship between the Australian state and Indigenous Peoples. He is an editor of *Global Citizens: Australian Activists for Change* (Cambridge University Press, 2008).

Tim Rowse is Professorial Fellow, Dean's Unit, School of Humanities and Communication Arts, University of Western Sydney. Since the early 1980s, he has been studying the history of Indigenous Australian contact with settler colonists, and in recent years he has included Canada, the United States, and New Zealand histories. The foci of his research have included public policy (its rationale and effects), the quantification of the Indigenous presence in official statistics, Indigenous political thought, and Australian Indigenous autobiographies. In 2012, Aboriginal Studies Press published his *Rethinking Social Justice: from 'peoples' to 'populations'*, and Routledge published a collection he edited with Lisa Ford, *Between Indigenous and Settler Governance*. He is working on a history of Australia's relationship with Indigenous Australians from 1911 to the present.

Note on Indexing

E-IR's publications do not feature indexes due to the prohibitive costs of assembling them. However, if you are reading this book in paperback and want to find a particular word or phrase you can do so by downloading a free e-book version of this publication in PDF from the E-IR website.

When downloaded, open the PDF on your computer in any standard PDF reader such as Adobe Acrobat Reader (pc) or Preview (mac) and enter your search terms in the search box. You can then navigate through the search results and find what you are looking for. In practice, this method can prove much more targeted and effective than consulting an index.

If you are using apps such as iBooks or Kindle to read our e-books, you should also find word search functionality in those.

You can find all of our e-books at: http://www.e-ir.info/publications

www.ingramcontent.com/pod-product-compliance
Lightning Source LLC
Chambersburg PA
CBHW072146020426
42334CB00018B/1908